At Least It's Not Raining

Stephen Redman

New Wine Press

New Wine Ministries
PO Box 17
Chichester
West Sussex
United Kingdom
PO19 2AW

Scripture quotations are taken from the following version of the Bible:
Holman Christian Standard Bible
Copyright © 2004 Broadman & Holman Publishing Group
New English Translation
Copyright free
New International Version. Copyright © 1973, 1978, 1984 Biblica.
Used by permission of Zondervan. All rights reserved

ISBN 978-1-905991-49-5

Typeset by **documen**, www.documen.co.uk
Cover design by CCD, www.ccdgroup.co.uk
Printed in the United Kingdom

Dedication

To Pauline - Simply the best wife, mother, and friend. You said the title and set the tone for our battle. We are still standing.

To Libby, Melody and Arielle - you are mature beyond your years and a great comfort to your mum and dad. You played your part in this story and came out shining. Only we five and God really know everything that happened and we can still feel it. Rocky will always be part of our lives.

CONTENTS

Foreword

In 2003 Irene and I found ourselves in a world we were not prepared for. Our 16 year old son David had just been diagnosed with an aggressive cancer at the back of his right eye and we were ushered into an oncology ward which would be our regular visiting place for months ahead. Through God's goodness, the prayers of the church and excellent medical treatment, David is now cancer free, is married to Sarah and recently a son Jackson has miraculously been added to the family.

When Stephen Redman asked to me to read through the story of Rocky's battle with cancer I put off reading the first chapter as I knew I would re-live some of the pain of our past experiences. I knew also that the Redman family's story turned out very differently from our own. I found the first few chapters to be a painful experience but the more I read the more I realized this was equally a story of God's goodness and grace. The family approached things from exactly the same perspective as our own and beyond the pain there unfolds a beautiful story of a brave boy who is now enjoying the greatest adventure of all. Books like this one need to be written and need to be read. Life doesn't always turn out the way we would want but behind it all is a loving Father who is working out His purposes for our ultimate good.

Stuart Bell.
Senior Pastor, New Life Christian Fellowship, Lincoln
Leader of the Ground Level Network of churches.

Introduction

In the UK we specialize in sanitising painful experiences. We wheel the sick and the dying away into designated spaces where no-one has to see. We prefer not to talk or even think about anything associated with pain or suffering.

We don't like pictures of suffering children, so we give generously when charity appeals use such photographs.

We don't talk about the painful past, and in general we try to pretend it didn't happen. We do not go back to places that remind us of pain or even where we might be made to feel uncomfortable.

Whatever our feelings or the threshold at which we become uncomfortable, children get sick. Thank God that not many of them do, but cancer is the largest killer disease of children in our society. We have grown up in the age of low infant mortality rates; we expect our children to grow to maturity and bury their parents.

Perhaps there will be 500 children in the UK who develop cancer this year.

Don't worry – it is OK, the statistics are that it will not come near you.

But what if it did?

This book is my story – the story of my family and particularly my lovely little boy Rocky.

You have no right to the information in this book – it is personal; by writing this I make myself vulnerable to you. Yet, the information on these pages is now in the public domain – I have willingly given you some insight into the Redman family.

I have chosen to write these things for a number of reasons.

Firstly, you have not had chance to meet my boy or get to know him. I would like you to have this opportunity. Hopefully you can get to know him through the pages of this book.

Secondly, our experience and the pilgrimage of my family have been significant to us. We are not ashamed, neither are we afraid to talk about our experiences. The window I am giving you on the lives of a family with a child with cancer will not just preserve our story, but perhaps it will help you to understand and have compassion on those who suffer around you.

Finally, God is good.

When I visit the children's cancer unit in Leeds I try to make a beeline for families with a new diagnosis. I remember that this time is especially difficult and I allow myself to be used as a dumping ground for their feelings if they wish.

The fact that amazed me at first is that people who have had no church background and lived their lives without any reference to God will immediately say 'How could God allow this to happen to my child?'

Without them knowing my role as a minister I find they ask *me* this question.

God gets some really bad press when children suffer. This book is written to demonstrate that in fact God is good. I would love you to take on board this one truth – because I have walked it out and found it to be true – God is a good God and not the author of our trouble.

I pray that you never have to walk the way we have. In reality though, we know that '*man is born to trouble as surely as sparks fly upwards*' (Job 5:7 NIV). We all come across difficulties in life – and they are all relative. I was once serving coffee and cake to parents when a man stormed in who was so angry that I thought he might hit me. I shoved a huge chunk of cake in his hand and asked him what had happened. He told me how he had just come up seven floors in the elevator with an old lady complaining of her bunions. That day he had been told his daughter had leukaemia and may not live. He proceeded to say that he had wanted to grab this lady by the throat and tell her to shut up about her bunions when children were dying in the building.

I asked God how to respond to him and the words that came out have helped me and others since. To this old lady her bunions were probably the worst thing that had ever happened to her. They caused her pain and the surgery was not nice. Relative to her position this trouble was as bad as it gets. To the man whose daughter was newly diagnosed his trouble was as bad as it gets too.

Trouble is relative – it feels bad when it is your trouble. Instead of becoming obsessed with our troubles which could stop us seeing someone else's need, we must share the comfort we have received with them.

Bunions are bad. Cancer is bad – *but God is good!*

Turn the pages with me and follow the trial and adventure of a sweet Yorkshire family. Perhaps by the grace of God you will be enriched by our journey and learn something along the way that will help you deal with your own issues. Whatever the outcome I trust you will rejoice with us, because of all families we are the most blessed.

1 *Life was Good*

There can be no doubt that we were enjoying life. Since Pauline and I fell in love and married fifteen years previously life had been a pretty good ride. That isn't to say that we hadn't known any difficulties; but we had learnt to enjoy ourselves whatever was going on around us. We had long since arrived at the mind-set that understands that we are a product of our own choices and some of those decisions carry a price tag. Some of the choices we had made together over the years had looked very strange to onlookers, but our friends had come to expect the "unusual" from the Redmans.

When it came to children, the age we live in dictates that to have one child is OK, two is still normal, three indicates inadequate precautions and four or more must be the result of poor mental development. We have loved each of our children and came to a time when we decided to have each one, so number four child was no mistake, but a clear result of choice.

In the delivery room, I remember crying when I realised that we had a boy. After three girls, we had just assumed that we would always have girls! Having decided on "Evangeline Destiny" as the names of our new baby, my tears were not just tears of joy, but recognition that I had brought a boy into the world without a having a name ready for him. We had always believed that names were special and had made careful decisions about them beforehand – we just didn't think we would have a boy.

We sat there cuddling him and discussing the meaning of various names that we knew. I had a hankering for "Rocky" – we talked about it and Pauline said that he looked like a "Rocky", so the name was chosen. His sisters all had a second Christian name and for Rocky we settled on the name "Josiah", which means, "whom God heals". We believe that God has the answer for every problem, including sickness, so it seemed appropriate to use this name. I remember it crossing my mind at the time "if you really believe this, then by giving your son this name will you have to prove you believe it?" Dismissing any doubt we settled on Rocky Josiah Redman, and discussed how good "R.J." would sound.

So it was that Rocky became part of our lives. He had four mothers – the girls loved having a brother almost as much as Pauline enjoyed having a son. I was busy building a new career for myself with the largest computer retailer in the UK, Pauline was busy home-schooling the children (I did mention that we made some unusual decisions). When we weren't doing our day jobs, we were involved in the church in one role or another. Pauline ran the kids-church programme and was continually writing material, whereas I was involved in the teaching side for the adult congregation.

Life continued on, as it does for all of us. My mother had been ill, and died in the autumn of 1998. With all the business of life, and handling my mother's affairs, we were blissfully unaware of the difficulties ahead. About a week after my mother's funeral Rocky started to be ill. We had prayed for him – and we believed this was the solution for the problem.

At first Rocky seemed listless and without interest in anything. He began to complain about aching joints and started to have the occasional temperature. Reasonably enough, we assumed this was just a virus and didn't involve a doctor as we couldn't see the need in pumping him full of antibiotics when he would just get better by himself. Indeed, that is exactly what happened – after about ten days he was better.

Warning bells first rang in my head when after being well for three or four days, he started again with the same symptoms. No runny nose, no coughing, just fevers and aching joints. For hours he would just lie on the couch and not move, looking pale. So I took Rocky to see our GP. Having explained that we were there because Rocky had got better but now had the same symptoms, our GP quite reasonably said that it was probably a virus and that Rocky was maybe a little run down and had caught a second virus on top of the first.

It was November 5th, and we were invited to spend "Bonfire Night" with some friends who lived close by. Although Rocky was not well, he obviously wanted to see the fireworks and we all went to visit our friends. Very soon it was clear that Rocky just could not stand outside with everyone else, so I sat in the house with him, watching the display through the patio doors. Disney's Toy Story was a popular movie at the time, and in this story a toy soldier is taped to a rocket by a little boy and launched into the sky. Our friends suggested that we do this as it brought back memories of a really fun movie. That night they let Rocky pick the soldier and he and I watched as this soldier was launched into the sky. That night will always be remembered for the fun we had with that poor toy soldier, but we also realised just how uncomfortable Rocky was, that he couldn't go outside to watch the launch.

Life continued with our little boy on the couch for a further two weeks after which he recovered. You can imagine our disappointment when after a few days he started with the same symptoms again. By this time it was the middle of November. I took Rocky to see the GP, who again could not see evidence of anything other than a virus. Our GP had commented in times past that it was a rare thing to see our family at his surgery; with this we were breaking the pattern. He took a blood sample and a urine test that seemed to confirm his diagnosis. Rocky was a little anaemic, which was indicative of being run down and susceptible to infection. He prescribed an iron supplement.

Days after with no change, and a realisation that Rocky wasn't eating and so was losing weight, we went to the doctor again. As excellent as he is, our GP could find nothing else and was about to send us home to "ride out the virus" when I asked, "Is there anything else we can do?" His reply was that he could call the consultant paediatrician at York District Hospital if I wanted, but that he hoped that I realised that if Rocky was referred to a consultant he would probably be kept in hospital overnight for tests. Contrary to every pattern I had previously established, I asked the doctor to do this. To this day I cannot think why I wanted the hospital involved, because in my heart of hearts I was convinced it was just a virus, but the words came out of my mouth seemingly without a conscious decision.

We drove straight to the hospital where Rocky was admitted for tests. There an excellent team of doctors poked and prodded him, testing him for meningitis, glandular fever and a host of things that I have forgotten now. In the early evening Pauline and I changed places so that she could stop overnight with Rocky. We had no idea that this was going to be our way of life for months to come.

The following day a theory was put forward that I bought into. Rocky, it was thought, had a human variant of psittacosis or parrot flu. Not only did the symptoms match Rocky's condition but on the afternoon of my mother's funeral he alone had been shown around his uncle's aviary which contained parrots! The fact that this explanation fitted the evidence won me over. Rocky's presence in hospital and the upheaval in our household, arranging someone to look after the girls whilst I worked, was unsettling. The sudden arrival of a simple explanation was a pleasant relief. The chart over his bed said that he had been admitted for "pyrexia of unknown origin". This simply meant that he had a temperature, but on Friday of that week they explained to Pauline that there were three possible scenarios:

◊   he would get better and they would never know why he had been ill,

◊   they would discover the source of the infection and treat it, or

◊   there was always the remote possibility that some type of leukaemia was involved.

They could not find the source of infection. Despite the fact that they had explained the possibilities, I was totally won over by the parrot involvement and quite peaceful about the whole saga. My wife needed a bit of consolation and I wrote off her concerns as being related to her previous history as a nurse and that mothers worry more! Rocky came home for the weekend and we enjoyed being together, until Monday morning when he returned to hospital to get the test results.

That Monday was November 30th 1998 and proved to be a day we were never to forget. I was managing an audit of the superstore I worked in – this was a key role and something I took very seriously. Pauline rang me towards the end of the day to tell me that they had been transferred to St James Hospital in Leeds. He didn't have parrot flu and this meant that they must test him for leukaemia. Rocky was on a cancer ward!

My mind was full of the audit. This was an important time for me – I had recently set up this new store and our first audit was a time of measuring how well I had performed. The personal statement that a good audit result made was important to me. Surely Rocky could not be seriously ill? Sick children are something you read about in the newspapers. My children couldn't possibly be affected by any-thing severe. We believed in God, and that he is a good God – we never fell for any of that "guy with a big stick" stuff. It was almost irrelevant that Rocky was in hospital, except for the fact that it was stressful for my wife. Rocky would be fine, but it was Pauline and my job that I had to focus on. At this stage it wasn't that I was in denial, I just could not conceive that this was a serious situation. Nothing of course was to be further from the truth.

I waited until the auditor was finished for the day before I went home. I collected my girls who were with friends and got them to bed before ringing Pauline. She obviously was troubled and we talked about leukaemia, which I strenuously denied as being a possibility. Pauline told me how awful it was on the ward, although at Jimmy's she was at least able to make a cup of tea.

As much as I really needed to be at work the next couple of days to manage the audit investigation, I contacted my line manager and explained that I needed to be at the hospital. He was more than understanding and asked me to keep him informed.

I felt like I was letting down my team at work, but I was acutely aware that my wife needed me. I didn't really think that there was anything wrong with Rocky, but I knew that we had a fight ahead – I just did not know that it would take so long or stretch our sanity the way it would.

That night I prayed out of confusion and bewilderment. I told God I believed in His healing power for my boy. I prayed for my wife that she would be able to cope with the horrible surroundings she was in, and I prayed for Rocky that he would soon be home and well.

2 *The Longest Week*

It was Tuesday the 1st of December. I had arranged someone to look after the girls and set off for St James Hospital in Leeds. I had no idea where to find it and took a wrong turn on the way (this was not unusual for me). I had to queue for over half an hour to get a car parking space, and then I went in every wrong building I could whilst trying to find ward ten. I was anxious, very concerned for Pauline, and I wanted to be at her side. I was confident that Pauline would have Rocky settled, as she always knew what to do for our children. I also knew from what Pauline said that the consultant wanted to talk to us together. This statement had an ominous ring to it.

I arrived at Ward 10, little knowing that it was to become our "second home". On arrival I was absolutely convinced we would be over this thing in a week. The sights of this ward were a terrible shock. Over the next nine months, there were many times when we were disappointed at the few people that were prepared to visit us, but the sight of all the suffering children was enough to disturb anyone. There was also an air of death and despond-ency about the place. The staff were good, and many charitable donations had been made to help make the ward brighter and more liveable, but these things could not counter the shock of seeing children who looked worse than old news reels of the Jews liberated from Belsen.

As I opened the door to Ward 10 I saw a little boy with one eye bulging out on his cheek. I later discovered that he had a tumour behind his eye, but it reminded me of a frightening episode of the Outer Limits that I had seen as a child, and a chill ran down my spine.

As I walked into the four-bedded unit that held my wife and son, a young girl was beating seven bells out of her dad. As she continued to thump him, he looked at me and just said "steroids". It was enough to tell me that as a side effect of the dose of steroids she was exhibiting violent behaviour. This sight did not inspire confidence.

Wherever I looked there were children who were bald, and had tubes in their noses and chests. Pumps on stands administering chemotherapy drugs that were "beeping" indicating a problem, and the regular sound of vomiting, were accompanied by the smells of full bedpans and a groaning that came from somewhere indistinguishable. Nurses were running around trying to keep a smile on their faces, but clearly pressured by lack of resources and grumpy parents they struggled.

My own son was on a drip.

A drip!

A needle was in his arm and liquid was being added to his blood-stream – this wasn't a stranger on a TV show – this was my boy.

I calmed myself.

This environment was a foreign place to see my wife and son. I met Jen who was to be Rocky's nurse for that shift and a regular face in the bleakness of St James. Pauline was desperate to talk to me. She wanted my company, but also to try and make me understand the seriousness of the situation. Pauline knew that I did not believe that Rocky was seriously ill, but always having a good handle on reality, she was going to get through to me.

Pauline talked much about what she could see around her, and also about what the consequences might be if Rocky really did have cancer. Emotions were high and we were in a place where we did not know what the future held.

The question that Pauline wanted to ask me was unspoken but I could feel its presence; "what if he dies?" I didn't believe this was an option, and Pauline was not panicking, but the question crept out without articulation, as the reality of where we were began to sink in.

The real horror that day was the trauma of having to deal with consent forms – the papers that had to be signed for tests to be conducted on Rocky. I had heard about horrible things going wrong with tests, and particularly with lumbar punctures. This, of course, was one of the procedures they wanted to conduct on Rocky. They also took bone marrow samples for analysis.

Rocky had an anaesthetic for the second time in his life. The first time had been a year before when he had stuck a small toy magnet in his ear. I think Rocky wanted to know if you put something in one ear would it come out the other? He soon found it wouldn't come out at all and he had to go down to theatre in York District Hospital to get it out. It was a procedure that lasted thirty seconds and had no side effects. This second anaesthetic was quite different. Pauline or I signed many consent forms over the next months.

Rocky was clearly even worse. Now unable to walk because of the pain in his legs he looked limp, weak and very pale. They told us that his blood count was low and were preparing us for thoughts of transfusion. I remember thinking about contaminated blood and HIV and NOT wanting a transfusion. I suppose I saw danger in the treatment, but of course Rocky's condition was in itself dangerous. If you are stuck on the top of a burning building sometimes the only way to survive is to jump – but no one likes the thought of jumping. The thought of pushing your child out of such a building is not pleasant, but if the chances of survival are better that way then you have to weigh the risks and make the judgement call.

We waited for test results and a visit from the consultant. The wait seemed eternal. When Mike came and sat with us at the end of Rocky's bed it was to tell us that there was clearly some abnormality but nothing conclusive. We could hope that it would be A.L.L. the most common form of leukaemia, as this had an excellent prognosis, but there were several other things it could be and we needed the results of the bone marrow test. This man was clearly as nervous talking to us as we were listening to him; there was something strangely comforting to me in this.

When I went home I had to ring my line manager to explain that I would be off work for at least the next week, whilst we found out what was wrong. I think I lost my composure for a moment and he realised just how serious the situation was. As a father himself, my boss was very understanding. He was one of the few people I found I could really talk to.

Around this time the few people who we really counted as friends were very visible – some looked after our girls and others were just there! My close friend Keith never failed to be there, ringing and visiting, but never getting in the way.

The next day Rocky had to have blood. When I realised how hard his heart had to work to keep him alive with such a low red cell count I knew that the risk of a transfusion was no risk at all; but it was not easy watching it happen.

We waited another eternity to see the consultant, and this time he took us into a room in which we would not be disturbed. I watched while he fumbled with the table lamp, trying to turn it on to produce an ambient light in the room. He nearly broke it and had to let the nurse fix it for him. His actions betrayed his own trepidation, and I knew the news was bad. He told us that they had found cancerous cells and it was not A.L.L. but that it could still be another form of leukaemia, which still had a 50% survival rate, although the treatment was more aggressive. He also said that it was possible that the cells had not originated in his blood, but had broken off from a tumour somewhere. This latter possibility would of course be the worst possible outcome. Whereas I don't remember it being said, there was a definite inference at this stage that there may not be any treatment available if this were the case. Mike left us alone to have a moment of quiet together. We cried.

I left Pauline in the early evening, picked up the girls from a friend's house and put them to bed. We weren't hiding anything from them and we were encouraging them to pray for Rocky, as indeed our whole church was praying. Our telephone was in the hall, and I tried to talk to Pauline sat on the bottom stair, but I became very aware that Elizabeth, our eldest, was listening. It was hard to be private and I remember deciding to go out the next day and buy a cordless phone so I could sit and talk to Pauline without prying ears. I also was starting to get very emotional whenever I spoke on the phone and struggled to answer it. I added a new answer-phone to the shopping list to filter our calls.

The next day, Thursday, Rocky was scheduled for a bone scan. Rocky was given a sedative for this test, as they were concerned as to whether he could lie still for a protracted period of time. Rocky didn't need the sedative and on future occasions never had one. We watched as Rocky was scanned from head to foot and then wheeled him back to the ward. When we returned to the ward our minister and his wife were there. We were pleased to see both of them – we were pleased to see anyone! I was acutely aware of how difficult he found it on the ward, but he insisted that Pauline and I go for a walk together whilst they sat with Rocky. As this was our first chance to be alone for days, we took it and walked out of the hospital around the grounds.

As we walked past reception, a courier was delivering the biggest teddy bear we had ever seen in our lives. We commented to each other how some child was going to be delighted with this wonderful gift. I also remember speculating how much a bear like that would cost: £100? £200?

We walked around the grounds. Events were happening at such a pace that we could hardly keep up. The pressure was high, and I talked a lot of rubbish. In all of this I do remember thinking and saying "God is good". Our circumstances were bad, life was hard, but God was good. This was probably the best thing I had ever said. We did at least know that God was on our side and that somehow there had to be some good coming our way. We did not waver in our belief, but instead put into effect the truths that we had been taught.

This wasn't time for panic but time for Papa – our Father God. We talked, we prayed, we cried, and we decided to carry on.

As we returned to the bedside, Rocky had been joined by the biggest bear in the world. That bear we had seen at reception had been for Rocky. It came with a card from my colleagues at work who had ensured that the courier sent a non-smoking driver and they swept out the van themselves before allowing the bear on board. When Rocky awoke he coined the name "Big Bear", which seemed appropriate. Our minister encouraged us with a story of some lepers in the Bible. In their time there was no food because an invading army besieged the land. They were faced with a dilemma – if they stayed where they were they would die of starvation – but if they surrendered to the enemy they would probably be killed. If they stayed they died, if they surrendered they might still die – this was not an easy situation. However they said "*let's go over to the camp of the Arameans and surrender. If they spare us, we live; if they kill us, then we die.*" (2 Kings 7:4 NIV) He said we must go on, because perhaps we may live! Indeed life was the very issue of the moment and the decision to go on was ours.

After the visitors left us, the Consultant Mike once again came to see us. This time he took us into the music therapy room, as it was the only *quiet* place that was empty. Fidgeting, he told us that Rocky did not have leukaemia, but that they suspected a solid cancer had spread to his bone marrow. The expanding bone marrow was causing his bone pain. This meant there was a tumour hiding somewhere in his body and the next day they were going to look for it. Mike would be handing us over to a colleague, Sue, who dealt with solid cancers.

By that night I had the cordless phone fitted so that I could talk to Pauline with less fear of being overheard. The calls from "well-meaning but stupid" people started. One call from a minister of another church suggested that Rocky was ill because I had done something wicked – I should repent! A woman suggested that an evil spirit from my mother had transferred to Rocky when she died. None of these unhelpful comments from the maladjusted did anything to make me want to answer the phone.

I was now very wary of the phone and started using the answerphone to screen all calls before I answered.

Instead of being reactive to the phone I started being proactive with email and by speaking publicly at church. I sent out emails each week to all who were interested to encourage prayer for Rocky and the family. I also stood up almost every week in the church to give news, raise hope and motivate others to pray.

For those leading prayer groups, I gave them notice in advance of meetings of the key needs and points for thanks.

We prayed as a family, we prayed with Rocky. I knew God answered our prayers but I was also convinced that when many agree in prayer it brings a result, so I was grateful for all the prayer support we had.

3 *Christmas Comes Early*

Have you ever thought "Maybe this is just a bad dream and I will wake up soon?" We were at that point. I was having to look after my girls, farm them out during the day, and then spend time at the hospital with my wife and son, in a sort of "no-mans land". We did not know what the outcome of these events would be, but at least we had hope. It was becoming clear that on Ward 10 we were the only ones with any hope for Rocky.

That Friday lunchtime we wheeled Rocky down to the ultra-sound scanning room. There they covered his abdomen with jelly and pressed the probe on him as they looked on the screen. My last experience of seeing this process had been when Pauline was pregnant with Rocky. Instead of seeing his picture on the screen, it was now his body that was being scanned and the shape inside him that was discovered was not a normal part of life, in fact it was nothing to do with life – something to do with death.

I couldn't make much sense of the screen, but it was obvious from the sudden activity and the call for Consultant Sue to come into the room that they had found something. This was the moment we met her – a person we came to appreciate very much.

It was only a matter of an hour or so before Sue came to see us to tell us what they had found.

Neuroblastoma.

What a word!

She explained that this type of cancer was not usually found in someone of Rocky's age. It was most commonly seen in children between 12 and 24 months of age. It occurs when the nerve fibres being produced as the body matures from infancy continue to be produced after the process should have ended. Rocky was 4½. Typically the tumours occur around the adrenal gland on the neck of the kidney, and in Rocky's case this was on the left gland.

She went on to label this neuroblastoma as a stage 4. She also told us there were 4 stages. This was to say the least, ominous. A stage 4 occurs when the cancer has spread into another organ. In this case there was clearly a spread into the bone marrow. Normally the cancer spreads to other soft tissue before reaching the skeleton and this may have meant that Rocky was riddled with the disease.

By this time we were starting to get the picture – they did hold little hope. To our great surprise, she went on to tell us that there was treatment that could be tried. We were amazed – we were convinced she was going to say that there was no treatment available. She talked about taking a biopsy of the tumour, which would be the first step. There are apparently tests that they can perform on a piece of the tumour to look for "good or bad genes". Those with a bad gene type have a low success rate and those with a good gene have a better success rate. The next step in the same operation was to fit a "dual Hickman line" in Rocky's chest. This led directly into the jugular vein and allowed easy access for blood products or chemo drugs. This would have to remain in until treatment was concluded and created its own issue in wound care and cleaning the pipes. After the operation chemo would start. There were to be 4 different chemo cocktails, which would be given in sequence, followed by a series of tests to check on their effectiveness. If there were signs of improvement another 4 cycles would be given which should hopefully clear the cancer from the bone marrow and other tissues, whilst reducing the size of the tumour ready for its removal. If no improvement were seen, then of course treatment would be discontinued. If treatment were to continue there were many risks from its toxicity which could also cause death or damage to organs. In addition to all this, the greatest actual risk was the suppression of the immune system – even the smallest infection could lead to death.

Sue was very good with us, but there was so much to take in, she gave us a piece of paper with the drug names on and scribbled some notes down for us – we still have this paper. She indicated that it was possible to have 16 cycles of chemo in parcels of 4, and that the process was a long one because there were 21 days between each chemo because of the body's need to recover after each treatment. It also appeared that there was a trial running where randomly patients were selected to have the same treatment at 10 day intervals. The downside was the body struggled much more with the toxicity and infections were more common, but the upside was the treatment was over a shorter period and perhaps getting the drugs in more frequently might attack the cancer cells more effectively.

We were left alone in that quiet room again. We sobbed together, not knowing how to process the information we had heard and the 'sentence' passed over our son's life. This was the worst that could happen, the lowest point in our lives.

It was at this most poignant of moments that two hopeful people who had just felt the rug pulled from under their feet looked into each other's glistening tear-filled eyes speechless.

It seemed like an eternity, but was probably only a few seconds. Pauline spoke the words that sounded trite, but were in fact the most powerful she could muster. "At least it's not raining", she said.

With all the pressure, the sight and smell of death around us and the declaration of death hanging over our son, my lovely wife was desperate to say something hopeful, and at least recognised that the low December sun was shining through the window.

"Yes", I replied, somehow knowing that if it had been raining it would have been too much that day. We had just enough strength to face that day together and not one drop more. Of course God had promised that *'As your days, so shall your strength be.'* (Deut 33:25 NKJV). My wife amazed me, inspired me and showed me hope with that simple sentence. We would be alright, we just had to sit tight and ride this one.

It was at this time that we invented the 'family meeting'. I suppose we had the first one when I got the girls together to tell them their Nana had died that October. Now however, we were having a meeting about Rocky. I sat the girls down and explained to them in words that they understood how ill he was. I explained that Rocky had a lump and that there was a possibility it could kill him. The next few weeks and months would be critical, but that we must pray and believe for a good outcome. I told them this was a fight – and that it was one we could win because God was with us.

This wasn't the last meeting we had this way, but one thing it did establish was that Mum and Dad were going to be honest with them and they knew that if there was something happening that they would be told. With hindsight we know from the girls that they appreciated this and that it gave them a lot of confidence.

Rocky was booked in for his biopsy and Hickman line for Monday December 7th. By now it was clear that we would be in and around Ward 10 for a long time. Obviously, we wondered how long it would be before we would ever be at home together again. Our answer came quickly, but not the way we were expecting. They came to tell us that we could all go home on Saturday afternoon and have Sunday at home, prior to the operation on the Monday. You would think that we would just be overjoyed to be going home. In a way we were but there was a sting in the tail of this weekend at home. They told us they would like us to go home and have Christmas, as it might well be our last Christmas together. To the reader "it might be" may not sound as bad as it did to us, because although the words were "it might be", the intonation in the voice was "it will be".

I spent the following morning buying a turkey with all the trimmings and having the most intense session at "Toys R Us" that I have ever experienced. All the Christmas shopping that would normally be done over a month had to be done in a morning.

Just a month before Rocky was ill, a dear friend of ours had been diagnosed with lung cancer. Peter was in his sixties and looked very poorly indeed. Offering no long-term hope, the doctors gave him nine to eighteen months to live. At the time, never realising how close this would come to me, I remember thinking 'which reading from the Bible would I want to hear if I was in his shoes?' The reading that came to mind immediately was from Psalm 91.

'He who dwells in the shelter of the Most High will rest in the shadow of the Almighty.' My only problem as I read this was the struggle reconciling that the Bible says that God is light – so how can light cast a shadow? I looked up the meaning of the original word and found that it meant "to hover". Suddenly I realised that what the Psalm meant was that God hovers over the person who draws close to him. In modern understanding, that which hovers is a helicopter. So I said to Peter, "at this time you need to know that the helicopter gun-ship of the Lord is hovering over you".

Only a little more than a month later I found that my family needed the helicopter gun-ship of the Lord. Therefore I decided that it was time to buy Rocky his first 'Action Man' toy – 'Action Man Helicopter Gun-ship'. I still remember how hard it was to find one, assemble and wrap it. But before I went to Jimmy's to pick them up, it was discretely hidden at home.

4 *First Christmas*

Christmas was always "magical" to me. I can still remember the Christmas when I was two years old. That year I was determined to see Father Christmas, so I hid at the top of the stairs to see when "he" would come. It was then that I saw my Dad arrive home from work and my mother say to him, "you'd better bring his presents in so we can fill his pillowcase". That was when I found out there was no such thing as Father Christmas. I found it vaguely amusing that adults played along with this whole Santa story. The fact that I knew there was no red suited miracle man and that the adults were trying to perpetuate the myth gave me a real sense of superiority. That Christmas day I had a sky blue pedal car with working headlights – it was wonderful. Santa or no Santa, Christmas was great.

Five years later when my Dad died, just in time for Christmas, it was still special. It took me a long while to believe my Dad was dead; for a while I expected him to walk back in to tell me there had been a terrible mix-up.

My mother had a nervous breakdown; she was institutionalised over Christmas because the doctor feared that she would commit suicide. I spent the season with her in a mental institution.

I sang carols to the inmates, the nurses gave up their common room so the doctors could erect a massive train set for me and I had a great time – such is the magic of the season. The fact that my Dad hadn't paid for the train set, and it eventually had to go back, didn't spoil anything. I spent many strange Christmases with my mother, all of which held something special. Despite her phobias and suicide threats, I have many wonderful memories of life with my mother, especially the great Christmases we had. Learning as a child that there was still a "Father" I could relate to – by that I mean God – really helped me come to maturity whilst living with a mentally disturbed mother.

When I married Pauline, my mother moved away from the area out of spite. On our fist Christmas Day together, she rang after lunch to wish us a Happy Christmas. I told her what a wonderful lunch Pauline had cooked for me – because I was proud of Pauline. My mother complained that her cooking was obviously not good enough for me, and before she hung up, she screamed that she was going to stick her head in the oven and gas herself. With great understanding, Pauline said that if I had to go over and check on my mother that would be fine. I reminded Pauline that I wouldn't have to make the journey, because my mother cooked with electricity!

With four children, we had marvellous Christmases. We never perpetuated the Santa myth, although we enjoyed the fun of the season. Pauline and I both thought that we couldn't lie to our children about an invisible Father Christmas and then expect them to believe in an invisible Father God. Our children enjoyed the secret joke that they knew there was no Santa Claus, but other adults seemed to believe in him. We still took them on Santa's Sleigh Ride, and we did everything that makes special memories for children – we just added the truth, and it didn't seem to take the shine off anything.

Every Christmas morning, on went the video camera and we all watched one at a time while every parcel was opened. One year, I was unemployed at Christmas and we had nothing. Three days before that Christmas, I suddenly remembered that months earlier we had invited another family for Christmas dinner – what were we to do? The following morning I was woken up by some friends offering us a huge turkey that they had been given and couldn't use. I went to the supermarket just before they closed on Christmas Eve and bought every other element of Christmas dinner for about one pound as they madly reduced prices to clear. We had the makings of a fantastic Christmas, but no presents for what were then two daughters. All Pauline and I had done for months was talk about getting Elizabeth and Melody a Karaoke machine. The only problem was that the one I wanted them to have was £99, and we had no money. Pauline persuaded me that we would be all right and late on Christmas Eve a rather large box was delivered by some friends. Yes, you guessed it, on Christmas morning my girls sang with the exact model we were going to buy. We had everything that Christmas.

Now it was December 6th 1998. Into our minds had been seeded the possibility that this would be our last Christmas as a family of six. It seemed really insane having Christmas early, but we did everything we would normally do. I was up early getting the turkey in the oven, the video camera was on, everyone had a heap of parcels, and all were happy with the contents. All eyes were on Rocky. He was clearly uncomfortable and looking very thin. But as he opened 'Action Man Helicopter Gunship', I had great hopes that this would not be our last Christmas together. It is difficult to think differently to the "guidelines" you are given. I have no problem with the way the hospital handled our situation – they did a great job, but by preparing us for the worst they were making it hard to hope for the best. This is obviously a difficult balance to strike, and in a world where the worst is often the result, one can understand why you are prepared in this way. Somehow in my spirit, I sensed that we were going to have more Christmases and I lived in hope.

Hope is a funny word. When we say "I hope so", we usually mean "I doubt it". In our language "hope" has become a tenuous thing, a vague sense, close to superstition. In the Bible, the word "hope" means "confident expectation" – this is almost the opposite of how we use the word today. I can't say that I was confident all the time, but a confidence was starting to rise within me that I could describe as "hope".

That day seemed very tiring, but also fulfilling. We gave our little boy a Christmas to remember, which was also a tonic to our girls.

It was really something to get your presents three weeks before everyone else! The only thing I had not managed to arrange was for an early presentation of the Queen's speech! Keeping as busy as we were that day helped us too.

Rocky was inundated with gifts and didn't know what to play with first, but play he did and it was almost normal.

This was also the first Christmas we had celebrated without my mother. Our children thought her eccentric, but she was always generous at Christmas. She was also a bit of a damp squib some-times, and the kids didn't seem to miss her. I couldn't help but think that it was a great blessing to have lost her before Rocky became ill. To have looked after her as well would have been impossible, but the knowledge that it would have been too much for her to bear was worse. To my mother, everything was always harder than it was for you. I remember how she cried for days when Kennedy was shot! To have known that Rocky was ill would have "set her off" on one of her moaning trips; the suicide weapon would have been loaded and ready to fire.

Amongst the other interesting events this Christmas was Rocky's developing interest in Star Wars. I can't say he had ever been bothered about the movies before, but he watched them in hospital and suddenly developed an interest in the characters. On this day we bought him some Star Wars toys and he played with them "forever".

It was a really good thing that above every bed in the children's cancer ward there was a small LCD TV. Children could watch many channels for free whilst awaiting treatment or being confined to bed. I think it was there on ward ten that Rocky developed his voracious appetite for movies and cartoons. The Cartoon Network became standard viewing, and anything to do with Star Wars was essential.

There wasn't a lot of rest for parents in hospital. If you can imagine most children were four to a bay and that means that there were four parents in the same bay. Whenever any child vomited (a frequent scenario) or any other problem surfaced, all parents were awake. The most significant noise was the pump alarm – every child had an electronic pump that was either giving them blood or chemo drugs or even feeding them. Pump alarms sounded at the end of each dose, or whenever a blockage occurred in the line. Whenever any pump alarm went off, everyone responded – even if they all sounded different it wouldn't have helped much because of the proximity of the other pumps. Therefore, parents were tired all the time. Although December 6th was Christmas, for Pauline it was a desperate attempt to doze. She was already very tired by this time, and we both knew that we were at the start of something, not at the end.

5 *Operation*

Christmas was over for now.

It was Monday morning, December 7th, and we had to get ready to go back into hospital. The concept of what was about to happen was so wild, scary and life changing that we could hardly take it in. We were going to take our little boy into hospital, where someone we didn't know was going to cut him open. There was a possibility that this would be Rocky's last day of life – this was a major operation and he was weak. It is really hard to get your head around signing the consent forms and the question went around in my head as to whether we should even go.

Clearly, Rocky needed help. As much as the next step was very invasive, I knew of no other course of action. We packed and set off for Jimmy's.

This time we were not on the cancer ward, but the nearby surgical ward. Rocky was prepped for surgery and we sat around the bed whilst the time for going to theatre approached. Friends were looking after the girls and Pauline was looking after Rocky and me.

We had to sign all these papers again and again. I felt like I was signing my boy's life away. It was easier signing my mortgage, marriage certificate and credit card bills than this – yet it was still the same scribble at the bottom of the paper. How strange that this same action could cause such different feelings?

There was absolutely nothing I had ever signed that made me feel like this before. The nurses put on a brave face and tried to make everything seem in control and normal. Somehow, I wasn't convinced.

I had a sense of Déjà-vu that took me back to the day I bought Pauline's engagement ring. We had spent hours looking all over the country to find the ring we had imagined, only to finally come across exactly what we were looking for in Nottingham! I loved Pauline with all my heart, but I knew that by buying this ring I had crossed a Rubicon. This step meant that I really was going to marry her. As much as marrying Pauline was all that I wanted, I still struggled that afternoon coming to terms with the commitment I was now making by giving her a ring which meant "when you look at this ring be reminded that I will marry you soon". Yes, it all sounds very corny, and a little over the top, but I don't apologise for the way I am. The struggle I had that day, signing the credit card docket for the ring, and sitting down thinking of the consequences, did not compare with the day I was living in now. Although I did not know the full meaning of the commitment I was making, at least it was towards someone I wanted with all my heart. This time I was committing someone else that I wanted as part of my life into a surgeon's hands. I guess this helped me realise that whatever I had written my name to, I could still commit my son into God's hands.

We went down with him to theatre; he didn't like having "the prick" in his hand, as they pumped the "magic milk" into him that knocked him unconscious. It is funny how the mind starts to justify circumstances at times like this. Rocky did not like needles. It had never been a problem until he needed them! As the hospital needed to take blood samples regularly and he had already been transfused with red cells and platelets, it was necessary to get easy access to a vein.

Every time a nurse wanted a vein, Rocky kicked up a fuss. Because it had been necessary to get blood regularly over the pre-vious few days, he had a cannula fitted. This was a plastic tube with a needle on that stayed in a vein, so that access was "on tap". Rocky hated having a cannula in and they had been taken out to come home, but two new ones had been fitted for the operation (one in each hand). The trauma for us in seeing him so upset whilst having a cannula fitted was awful. Rocky had to have this done! And so we persevered with him as he screamed and wriggled. There were local anaesthetics available that could be rubbed on the skin before the process, but they didn't seem to make any difference at all to Rocky.

When fitting the cannulas for the operation, the nurse had said that at least after the procedure we would not have to subject Rocky to this again. The dual-Hickman Line would at least mean Rocky did not need injections or cannulas. The downside of the line was that it needed to be kept clean and dry. There would be no swimming whilst the line was in place! This somehow seemed a surreal comment. You will be familiar with the feeling you have when you are driving on the motorway at a crawl of 30mph and the electronic signs tell you to slow down to 50 mph? That is exactly how we felt when told that Rocky could not go swimming. Somehow in the size and scope of what was going on, swimming was the least of our worries.

The thought that there would be no more injections for Rocky to be upset by was some bizarre comfort as he fell asleep and we were ushered out of theatre. We prayed. We prayed that we would see him again, alive. We prayed that the biopsy would go well. We prayed that we would survive until he woke up.

This was the longest day.

We went for a drink at the canteen; it was uncomfortable and nothing tasted right. We walked around the grounds – the journey was over so quickly and nothing was of interest. We went back to the ward to wait – nothing there did anything to settle us or capture our interest. We went to the hospital shop and browsed the books, the sweets and the greetings cards. It all seemed so pointless. We went back to the canteen for something to eat but nothing on the menu was remotely appetising.

Were we totally ruled by anxiety? No. But we were impatient for a result and to see our little boy again. We knew the day would pass, but it dragged all the same. We were impotent. There was nothing we could do. Thank God that we could at least talk to him – and to each other. I think it was at this time that I first realised what a horrendous position this must be for a single parent – not having anyone to talk to and share those intimate thoughts.

The day dragged along, and as it became later and later, we expected to hear that Rocky was in recovery. As we waited by Rocky's empty bed on the ward, the surgeon, Mr Stiles, suddenly appeared at the door with a beaming smile. We had been told a nurse would call us to the recovery room, but in fact the surgeon had removed his scrubs and raced over to the ward to speak to us himself. His obvious smile removed the trepidation of the visit, which could easily have been taken the wrong way. After almost ten hours in surgery, he was able to tell us that he had fitted Rocky with a dual-Hickman line and because of the appearance of the tumour, he had been able to remove it along with the left adrenal gland that it was attached to. He went on to describe how his hands had "been all over Rocky's internal organs" and there was no sign of cancer anywhere else in the "soft tissue". Because it was so clear, he had decided whilst Rocky was on the table to remove the whole thing! Rocky was in recovery and doing well! We were allowed down to collect him.

Up to this point there hadn't been a hint of hope from the medical profession. This is not to say anything negative about them, they were just preparing us for the worst and clearly expected it. They had expected Rocky's organs to be riddled with cancer, but not so! This surgeon had come to tell us himself, because he believed it was good news, and so it was. His assurance that he had personally inspected Rocky's organs seemed incredibly comforting. We couldn't see inside our son, but this man had done, and what he had seen was better than what he had expected.

The plan had been to biopsy the tumour, then shrink it with chemo-therapy and remove it in a year or so. Now the plan was changed, and it all seemed to be working for us. Knowing that the tumour had gone was very encouraging. If you can imagine hiding under the bed-clothes, because you knew a burglar was in the house, then suddenly finding he was gone, this was how we felt. Rocky was still very ill, and without further intervention would still die in a little while, but that horrible invasive tumour was gone!

It is very difficult to describe the waves of relief that we felt. I felt relieved, enjoyed the feeling and then it would hit me again and again – all at different levels, but each time I felt "rescued". I was also consciously grateful to God. This had been a hard day to live through, but we had made it. The looks I exchanged with Pauline expressed more than words could and it was with great excitement that we raced down to recovery to see our little boy.

Rocky was the only patient in recovery, there was just the one bed with a little form on it. We came close to him and each reached out a hand so that we could feel the warmth of his body. He was sleepy, but awake. He was groggy but also clearly relieved and pleased to see his mother's face.

They showed us the wound. He was cut at about waist level and almost half way around his body. There was a pipe leading out of his chest that split into two. There was also a scar just above his collar-bone where the Hickman line entered his jugular vein under his skin. I saw these "invasions" into my little boy and I wanted to scream out. I wanted to cry on the spot that my little 'fella' had these horrible marks, but those tears were overtaken by the tears of joy when I saw him smile. This was a very good day. As Pauline told him that they had removed "his lump", she was clearly running on adrenaline and not knowing what to say next. The great thing about Pauline was that when I didn't know what to say, she always managed to come out with the right words – a mother's words.

We accompanied Rocky back with the porter as his bed was pushed back to the ward where he was living. The stress of the day made us feel very tired, but whether either of us would sleep was another question. To sit at the side of Rocky's bed and just look at him was a dream come true. To see his chest rise and fall as he breathed was a great comfort and joy. Normally, not one of us would think about breathing or look for the signs of it on each other, but today it was a simple joy to see him breathe.

I remember Rocky lifting an arm in the air and shouting "my lump has gone" when we told him. There was a zipper mark half way round his body but he was still happy about something.

It was time for me to go home and look after my girls. We had seen our boy through the day together, now Pauline was left alone with him and I was to make the journey back home. There were many days when I thought that we were blessed to live so near to Leeds and St James', but even the 23 miles seemed a huge gulf when I wanted to be with my boy. This was a struggle for our girls too – they loved Rocky – and so the responsibility fell on me to go and comfort them and encourage them that this was good news and to assure them that they could see him soon.

Like most nights, I finished the day by talking to Pauline on the payphone in the corridor of Ward 10. It wasn't ideal, but it was just so good to share our hearts with each other and at least be able to talk before trying to sleep.

6 *An Egyptian River*

It is my observation that, on the whole, men deal with the news of a child with cancer very differently to women. Everyone is upset, but in general women switch into coping mode and get on with the job of looking after their child. Men, however, have a tendency to take a long ride up a winding river called denial.

One dictionary defines denial as a "refusal to believe". As someone who strongly believes in an invisible God, a risen Jesus who overcame death and a comforting Holy Spirit, you would think it unlikely that I of all people would refuse to believe.

After all, belief is a choice.

We may choose to believe that a person cares about us, that the government have our best interests at heart and that what appears on the BBC news *must* be true.

We may choose to believe that it is worth paying £1 more for our coffee at a different shop because of the brand and that we need to have more sex because everyone else is doing so.

I have definitely chosen to believe in God, despite coming from a non-Christian home. My mother wanted me not to go to church and to be a "normal boy". I remember her saying that if I came home drunk having got some girl pregnant, "at least you would be normal".

Having lost my father when I was seven, my search for another Father took me to the doors of a church. I was cynical and questioning, but I couldn't escape the truth that I found out about myself; I needed forgiveness and a relationship with God. I tried desperately not to believe, but one day I made the choice and have never looked back since.

I heard that I had failed God and needed forgiving. I also heard that forgiveness was all accomplished by Jesus at the cross. All that I needed to do was to call on Father God, in the name of His Son Jesus; that would be my new start.

An invisible God, whose existence seemed beyond the possibility of scientific proof, became visible to me by faith, when I chose to look for Him.

So when I started my walk into ward ten, it was with a personal God and an understanding that He was good. However, I was hampered by my great resistance to the thought that this terrible thing could really be happening.

Our family seemed perfect. Our lives were great. My son was a delight. We were all healthy and it was my belief that nothing would change on that front.

I have had to fight in a negative world (and often in negative churches) to accentuate the positive. To believe for "good" when surrounded by "bad" has been a life-long fight! Many battles in our lives have been won by refusing to accept that all was lost in the same manner as Abraham. The Bible says of him that he believed in:

"the God who gives life to the dead and calls things that are not as though they were"

(Rom 4:17 NIV)

Unfortunately, in this case, I was not recognising the reality of the situation and trying to talk it away; almost believing that I could go to sleep, wake up and find it would all be over.

I struggled to come to terms with the changed reality. Cancer wasn't something that I could talk away. I needed to be positive and so did my family, but the real positive is when you recognise the reality and still believe!

The scars on my son's body were probably the strongest factor in dragging my brain into the real world. Being able to encourage my family to make a positive stand for life was going to be crucial over the next season in our lives. Not facing facts was not going to help – it would have made me ineffectual.

Even men who don't know God often find that their first stop on this journey is denial. It is often a 'guy thing' because we men like to believe we have a grip on what is happening around us and we refuse to believe anything different.

In the days of Moses, a wicked Pharaoh ordered the Jewish slaves to throw their male children into the Nile. The Nile was the source of life in Egypt; from it came water and irrigation for the fields. The Egyptians worshipped the Nile as a god. Throwing the Jewish boys in the Nile wasn't just a method of population control – it was an act of worship to the gods of the Egyptians.

The mother of Moses knew the penalty for non-compliance, and yet she refused to either worship the Nile or lose her precious little boy. Instead, she remembered how Noah had been saved from the floods by an Ark and so she made one for her baby. Because she refused to accept the status quo and did not allow the flow of the Nile to determine her family's future, the destiny of all Jews was changed.

Moses survived.

I was determined that my son would survive too. If I had to build an Ark of faith around him I would, but I would do it in the face of reality and not by denying he had cancer.

Somewhere around this time I woke from my stupidity and began to be there in the way that Pauline needed me to be. I encouraged my family and together we fought for life, believing in one who has already conquered the grave.

Now I was of some use.

Pauline was relieved.

7 A Time to Heal

At this time Rocky had to recover from a major operation. It is amazing how many factors the medical staff have to weigh up when treating children like Rocky. They had to leave just long enough for the wound to heal, but had to start chemotherapy as soon as practically possible. Chemo was essential to deal with the remaining cancer cells in the body, and in Rocky's case the secondary cancer in his skeleton. By this time tests had revealed that his entire skeleton had been invaded by cancer cells – except for his feet.

Parents have so many hurdles to get over in cases like these. Chemo is a very nasty treatment; it nearly kills all of your cells in the hope that it will kill the cancerous ones! It isn't just one chemical, but there exist a range of different chemo drugs which are made into cocktails and given in specific cases. The trial that was running, governing the time between drugs, was random; this decision was made centrally, not at the hospital. Pauline and I discussed this and felt that 10 day gaps would be better as there may be some benefit to Rocky as the treatment was more intensive. Also the likelihood would be that our stay in hospital would be shorter. There could be "swings and round-abouts" with this trial though. Children could go home in-between chemo cycles and only had to come back in if they caught an infection. Shorter gaps between cycles made it less likely that we would get home, as Rocky had to be over the worst before they would let him out. If he didn't recover well after a chemo, we could easily be in hospital for the full ten day gap.

We decided we wanted the trial, so we prayed.

Rocky was selected for the trial. However the first ten days were not for chemo, but for healing. My little boy needed time to recover from having his "lump" removed before they started with the toxic waste. So for ten days, Rocky learned to get used to cartoons on tap and a lot of cuddles with his mum, who spent more time in Rocky's bed then anywhere else. It was the best place to be.

Something had happened.

Two weeks earlier we had arrived in this alien ward, strangers in a strange land. Now, only a matter of days later, we are starting to become residents.

Sociologists tell us that it takes about three weeks to get so used to a dripping tap that you no longer feel any urgency to get it fixed. I know that it is possible to get used to an inconvenient drip, but I never dreamed that it was possible to become accustomed to a place like the children's cancer unit.

We were starting to get used to the place.

The kitchen at the end of the corridor was the social centre of the unit.

Most children's wards don't allow hot drinks, but the wise staff at St James knew that the parents living on the ward needed to be able to make a meal and to drink plenty of tea and coffee.

It was inevitable that when you went down to the kitchen to make a cup of tea, you would meet another parent and get talking about life, the universe and everything.

Pauline and I discovered other parents whilst being in a four bed bay, but we really got to know them in the kitchen!

Meanwhile Rocky discovered PlayStation.

In 1983 when Pauline and I were married, I sold lots of my stuff to buy essentials with. One thing I got rid of was my Atari VCS game console. My "Space Invaders" cartridge went with the console. Our second Christmas together we weren't quite as hard up, so Pauline bought me a new one. From time to time we would play with it and, as newer generations came out, I stayed with my Atari. In time it was relegated to the loft.

By the time PlayStation had come along, graphics were very different, but we were an unusual family in that we didn't play electronic games – we played board games.

On Ward 10, however, PlayStation was a literal God-send. When you are too ill to get out of bed, the idea of being able to play something exciting is appealing to kids. Rocky became very attached to "Crash Bandicoot" and whenever he was allowed, and there was a unit free, he played.

Because PlayStations were in limited supply and all the children wanted them, those who were well enough would often gather around each other's beds to share games and to watch in hope that they could get a turn.

This way, Rocky started to make friends with other children on the ward, and, as any parent knows, when your kids make friends you end up meeting and getting to know their parents too. In the confined environment of this special unit, it was an even more noticeable effect.

The other social pressure was the common status shared by parents. None of us had ever dreamed that we would have a child with cancer and for all of us our lives were on hold. It was as if a hand had appeared out of the sky and plucked us all up and dumped us in a foreign prison.

The commonality of our predicament had an amazing adhesive quality – bringing people together because no-one outside understood.

Starting to adjust the rhythm of life to this new and unwelcome situation, Pauline was coping like the hero in an epic poem, and I had awoken from my dream and had my feet in the real world again.

Now we were about to embark on another journey, one that would take us in the footsteps of many who lost their lives in the trenches of the First World War. Chemotherapy was developed from the mustard gas that cost so many lives in that conflict. We were about to inflict these toxins on our little boy in the hope that we might win the war against cancer in his body.

It is bizarre that we had spent the last four and a half years keeping him safe from any form of poison, and now we were signing consent forms for him to have them pumped into his body.

The irony was enough to make me laugh!

8 *Toxic Broth*

Part of the daily routine was now to maintain the dual Hickman line hanging out of Rocky's chest. The wound had to be cleaned with sterile wipes, and we had to make sure that the line was working. It is strange seeing your child with an artificial construct hanging out of his chest, but there was a sense of necessity that was starting to become a driving force in this mad time.

Rocky had to be topped up with red blood cells and platelets, but then this was now becoming just an ordinary part of life. Thank God for the generous blood donors who gave something of themselves to save my son!

The blood was regularly administered to Rocky through his Hickman line. As a believer in God's new covenant (an agreement brought into being through the blood of Jesus to save our lives), the sight of blood was a continual reminder that we were dependant on God above and beyond the advanced medical services and the kindly blood donors.

We prayed the efficacy and the healing power of the blood of Christ over our son whenever we saw blood products. My son's life was hanging on because of the blood. Without red cells and platelets he would die in days. As his red count fell, his heartbeat quickened. This strain was not good on a weakened body and needed to be rectified through the blood of another.

At the last supper Jesus said: *"This cup is the new covenant in my blood, which is poured out for you"*(Luke 22:20 NIV).

The blood of this covenant is the same of which Isaiah said *"He was pierced because of our transgressions, crushed because of our iniquities; punishment for our peace was on Him, and we are healed by His wounds"* (Isa 53:5 HCSB).

Our hope was in the covenant that the blood of Jesus made. Just as we took communion together as a family to remember the Lord's death, when we saw the blood of another being held up above the body of our son, we were reminded that real life comes from Jesus.

Chemo began.

So did the vomiting.

By now Rocky had lost a lot of weight and was starting to look painfully thin. The concept of him now vomiting up the little food he ate was disturbing. Anti-emetics, or as the kids called them, "anti-sick" drugs, were the other cocktail that Rocky was exposed to. On the first cycle of chemo they didn't help at all, but by the second they really did bring it under control.

By now Pauline had a first class degree in mopping up bodily fluids. Her nurse training was coming to the fore!

Hydration was a part of chemo – they would get plenty of fluid into him intravenously. This would make him look like he was putting on weight but it was only fluid in the tissues.

It was at this time that Rocky acquired his first piece of jewellery – a nose tube. To give it the correct title, a "naso-gastric feeding tube" was fed up his nose and down into his stomach. He had to be awake for this process because they needed him to be able to swallow it. The tube was attached to his cheek with a sticky substance and a cap was put in the exposed end, to be removed only when in use.

Rocky did not like having a tube fed into him this way. Rocky had nurses that he preferred to do this and ones that he didn't. Right at the beginning of his treatment a wonderful nurse called Mark had bandaged his cannula and Rocky was not happy with how it felt. Afterwards the nurse was always known as "Rough Mark". Although that hadn't been a great experience for Rocky, Rough Mark was often called to feed in a new NG tube. The problem with

NG tubes is that you have to make sure they are in the stomach and not in the lungs. A check is made every time before use with a syringe pulling up some liquid. A litmus paper test is conducted to make sure it is stomach acid that has come out the tube.

The other problem with an NG tube is that when you are vomiting it is difficult to not vomit the tube out! Consequently Rocky had a large number of NG tubes. Sometimes they only lasted one day, other times we would get away with a week.

After some training with the nutritionist, we were feeding Rocky when asleep with a liquid food from cans. The aim was to get as many calories into him as possible; we usually aimed for 800 a night.

Sometimes Rocky would throw up the lot; other times he would tolerate the night feed. Either way it helped us to slow down his weight loss and eventually stabilise it.

We had a pump to attach to his NG tube and after he had fallen asleep we would start the infusion, with the aim of getting 2 or 3 cans into him before daybreak.

The chemo itself was manageable with the anti-sickness drugs, but the real bite was when his counts began to fall. One result of the treatment was a fall in neutrophils – his white cell count would fall and his immune system would bottom-out.

When his neutrophil count was low (as low as zero) Rocky had no natural immunity, so any infection could be a risk. Chickenpox or measles could easily be fatal, but so could many other infections if they were allowed to get out of control. Ensuring Rocky did not knowingly come into contact with infections from the outside was always a concern, but what couldn't be guarded against were the bacteria that live inside the body – primarily in the gut.

After chemo it was a ten day wait for another cycle. During this time, if Rocky's vitals were fine and he had no temperature we could go home. The issue was that, with no immunity, Rocky could just catch something from his own body! We then had a 60 minute protocol to get him back into St James in that hour.

We were very blessed that we had the chance to go home again a couple of days after chemo. At home we had to make sure we had a digital thermometer and that we checked him regularly. If his temperature was above normal we had to check again in 15 minutes. If it was still high then we had to phone the ward to tell them we were on the way.

When we moved to York I remember saying to Pauline that we ought to live on the Leeds side of the city, because it would be an advantage. I guess I was thinking about employment possibilities, but what a huge advantage it gave us for Rocky. We were 23 miles from door to door and could always make it in 35 minutes.

The first time Rocky had chemo, we lasted one day and then had to go back into hospital. His toys, clothes, medicines and feeding pump had to go home with us.

At least we were all home again for one day!

When Pauline had been pregnant and near delivery we had learned to keep a bag packed and ready in the boot of the car. Now it was time to live this way again – one never knew whether we would need to set off back for hospital at any time.

We were waiting for the toxic river to do its job.

9 *Everything I Ever Did*

America, land of dreams – for those who make good, there is success; and for those who don't, there is Hollywood!

I had never been to America and didn't really know anyone from there, except for meeting a small number of preachers over the years who had visited England. I think it was in 1995 that I heard a man called Paul preach in York. He told us how God had preserved his life after he had been shot.

There was something about this man that I liked and, just once, I wrote to him at his church in Little Rock, Arkansas. I had no answer and very much forgot about him.

Long before Jimmy's, in 1996, I began to sense a need inside me to visit the USA that culminated in me having a dream about preaching in the church that Paul led. When I awoke, I heard what I had come to understand was the voice of God say to me that there were some things I needed to learn in that church. The voice also said that I was to visit Tulsa Oklahoma on April 18th at 4.30pm.

Yes, sometimes I hear a voice!

It was March, and I was in a job that I wasn't enjoying – it involved a lot of sitting around and doing nothing! I had applied to a national computer retailer to manage an out-of-town superstore, and they had offered me a position.

I resigned from the company I was working for and was left with a 3 week window of opportunity between leaving one job and starting the other. Pauline told me to go to America – as this was my opportunity.

The start date in my new job was the week after the 18th of April, so the date was a possibility.

I went to the travel agent and bought a ticket to Little Rock, then on to Tulsa.

I don't do crazy things every day – they are just as hard for me as for anyone else. This trip was just something I had to do and it meant leaving Pauline at home with my four lovely children for almost two weeks.

I wondered if this trip was about becoming a full time minister in the church, but it was just wonder. If I was honest, I hadn't got a clue what was going to happen; I just knew it was important.

I found the phone number for the church that Paul led and rang up. When I eventually got hold of him I introduced myself and said I wanted to go over and see him. He was very bemused and gave me "20 questions" as to why. He tried to put me off but I insisted. He then hit me with his diary and explained that even if I came, there was no way I could spend any time with him as he had three different visitors coming over.

I told him that if he could arrange a family in the church to put me up, then I would go to Little Rock and wait for an opportunity to see him. If I only had an hour with him over the next 10 days I told him that it would be fine. He reluctantly agreed, so I packed my case.

Before I set off, the church prayed for me and someone gave a prophetic message to me. They said "You are going to learn how trees multiply and bring that truth back to the church". What an obscure message!

The day to leave England came and as I sat on the runway at Manchester airport, I was talking to an American who lived in England and was on his way home to visit family. He asked me where I was going and as the aeroplane accelerated down the runway, with the engines screaming, he said "So you are going to Arkansas – the tree farming capital of the USA."

I was taken aback by this throw-away comment and told him that I was hoping to find out how trees multiply. We hadn't got as far as 2000 feet off the ground before he had told me that all you do with trees is "plant them close together and the wind does the rest". I pondered the relevance of this to church and enjoyed the journey.

Having taken the train to Manchester, and changed planes at Atlanta, I arrived at Little Rock about 23 hours after I set off from home. I was very tired but was met at the airport by a guy who ferried me straight to church as there was a meeting on.

The leaders of the church then took me out for a meal so they could talk to me. I don't know how coherent I was by this time, but they were a great bunch of guys. It became instantly clear that another man from England had been over a couple of years before, seeking employment in the church, and he had not been welcome. They had been suspicious of me, but it seemed that they were won over by my genuine sincerity.

The following morning Pastor Paul called me and said that the three sets of people that were coming to see him over the next ten days had all cancelled and his diary was now absolutely free. He picked me up and we drove around and talked.

I asked him about the trees.

In York, everyone has a hairdresser they call their own. It seems that in Little Rock, everyone has an allergist. The trees that are wind pollinated so surround the city that their fragrant pollen is an allergy issue to the local inhabitants. Whilst there, I would get up and eat breakfast outside on the terrace in the warm morning sun, enjoying the same fragrant air that caused allergies in the locals.

Paul explained to me that in the church he led, the leaders were all friends – they met each weekday for lunch and dealt with things as they arose. They didn't have any relationship issues because they saw so much of each other. This was an alien concept to me because in my church experience there was friction between leaders and no social interaction at all. This was probably because the senior leader of the church was a very private and withdrawn man who didn't like people very much – but this made effective church leadership difficult.

I very quickly felt that I had learned what I needed to know about how trees multiply and its relevance to church – I had to go back and try and re-engineer relationships.

I had a string of great days with Paul and the other guys at Little Rock, but there was one man missing. Everyone talked about a big guy called Johnny. He had an office in the church and the sign on the door said "Prophet".

Everyone seemed to revere the man and still I had yet to talk to him. I had seen him on Sunday because I watched him go up to a woman and her daughter who were visiting the church (of about 300) for the first time and say to the daughter "when were you going to tell your Mamma about the abortion?" The mother got very angry that he had accused her virgin daughter, but the girl blubbered and said, "I'm sorry, Mamma, I should have told you".

You could have knocked me over with a feather!

In my dream I had preached at the church, but during my stay no-one had asked me to do this. The last day that I was there, I asked if I could preach that night and was given the go ahead. Whilst waiting for the evening meeting, Johnny turned up and collared me. He took me into his office and put a 90 minute cassette tape into a recorder on his desk and began to prophesy to me.

He started by telling me that my father had died when I was seven and that my wife's father had died when she was young too, but not the same year. He told me what my mother did next and what my wife's mother did too. He told me how many children I had and what sex they were. He told me a number of very specific facts about myself that no one could possibly have told him and carried on with details about Pauline too.

He told me that we had one car but that my wife had been saying that she could do with one for herself, but that I had said we couldn't afford it. He told me to buy it on credit and that we would have to make some of the payments but not the majority. He told me that one of my daughters kept asking for a pet and that I had to stop being selfish and let her have one.

He went on to tell me that God was calling me to plant a church in England. He said that God had spoken to me and told me to go somewhere else after Little Rock. He seemed to know that I was expecting to meet someone significant there but he explained that two things would happen to me in this place. I would go to a place where I could see the whole city skyline and there I would prophesy to that city. He said that God would show me the root of a problem in City Hall.

The second thing that I would do whilst I was in Tulsa would be to have a day alone with God. He would then reveal to me His purpose for the next season in my life.

He also told me a selection of things about what my children would grow up to do. He struggled over Rocky, but said that he saw him playing rugby.

Like the woman at the well in the fourth chapter of John, I could say "I met a man who told me everything I ever did".

With my tape in my pocket and the words I had heard flapping in my mind like gulls around a seaside fast food stand, I said my goodbyes and took a plane to Tulsa.

I was terrified. At least at Little Rock there was a man I had heard of. I knew no-one in Tulsa.

A woman on the plane was leading a team of people in some sort of pyramid selling scheme. They were going to a conference in Tulsa. She asked me if I wanted to be involved, wondering if my reason for coming to Tulsa was to see her. I wondered too, but let it pass.

As I walked through the airport concourse a member of staff approached me and said "you are from England aren't you? How many children do you have?" I answered "4" and he told me to wait a moment. I waited many moments but he never came back. Weird?

I checked into a motel and cried. I rang Pauline and said that I didn't know what to do and she told me to pray. I looked in the yellow pages and discovered a number of churches whose ministers I had heard of. It appeared that Tulsa was headquarters to a number of well known Christian ministries. I thought I would ring them and ask if they had any meetings on, thinking I might meet someone.

It was Thursday, I rang six churches. All of them told me that there was nothing happening in church before Sunday – I was flying home on Saturday.

In desperation I looked down the page and saw "Oral Roberts University". I had heard of this and hadn't realised it was in Tulsa. I rang the campus and explained that I was visiting from the UK and asked if there was anywhere I could go to pray. They told me they had a prayer tower and asked me to come along and pray over the city. I called a cab and found I had a 45 minute ride ahead of me.

Once there, I entered this huge prayer tower. I came out of the elevator into a room full of people milling around as they looked at the view and prayed. I became aware that from here I could see the full skyline of Tulsa.

I was only there a few seconds when everyone suddenly left. I was alone in the room. I figured that this strange quiet in the room was for a purpose so I went over to the window and began to pray. As soon as I started I saw a vision (like watching a movie). In it were two men in suits – one grey, one brown. One was in charge of transport policy in the city, and I began to see the details of the corrupt activities that they were involved in – almost like I had CCTV. I prayed over the city regarding this issue and then stopped. I opened my eyes and a loud chime came from the elevator. The doors opened and people rushed out. Quiet had gone; it was now time for me to move on.

At 4.30pm I found a man who wanted advice on travelling to the UK and I prayed with him. We talked, exchanged contact details and I believe I helped him. He was black and used the title Bishop. Big deal?

Each of the churches I had rung had told me there was nothing on in Tulsa before Sunday, but there, next to the prayer tower, was a huge sports stadium. In it, tens of thousands of black Christians were meeting. I walked into the huge congregation. It seemed as if all eyes turned on me – the only white face. I turned in my tracks and left immediately. Then I realised that segregation hadn't died in the deep south. Black churches and white churches barely recognised each other.

I went back to my hotel room with a tub of "Rocky Road" and tried to take it all in. It was the next day that I spent entirely in prayer, and there I believe that God called me to plant and lead a new church. I came away with many notes from that day which have guided my life since.

When I got home I started to look into buying a second car. By the time I got it on a four year loan, we had to pay one year of payments and then my mother died and my share of the estate cleared the debt.

I fought the next one, but when Melody next asked me for a pet (I hate pets!) I bought her Speckle the much loved rabbit. No one would ever have believed that Stephen Redman would buy a pet!

As a couple, our plan was that I was going to plant a new church and that it would be founded on strong relationships. I would eventually follow the plan I had been given in a motel room in Oklahoma.

Little did we know that all these plans would have to be shelved because of the impending sickness of our son. When Rocky was ill, however, the idea of him growing up enough to play rugby became a focal point of hope for us.

Someone bought him an England Rugby shirt, another bought him a ball, and still another 'photo-shopped' a photo of a rugby player to put his name on the shirt. We began to talk Rugby – a sport that had never even interested us before.

When she married me, Pauline told me that if we had to live out of a suitcase she would do it. Ward 10 sort of fulfilled that, but not in the way we would have expected. At our wedding I had declared '*as for me and my house, we will serve the Lord*' (Josh 24:15 NKJV).

Dreams and visions seem fanciful stuff, but they cannot be ignored when facing the challenges of life. We were the Redmans, and first of all we would serve the Lord.

Had this trip to the USA been relevant? I think it had. Above anything else it confirmed a long felt call to the ministry in my life and the hand of God on us as a family.

Was the "unusual" part of our lives? Certainly, but we never expected cancer.

10 *The Second Christmas*

Time was dragging. Every second seemed like a minute. Every minute seemed like and hour, every hour seemed like a day.

We were never sure whether Rocky would live through the day – Christmas was approaching and we could not get out of our minds that we had not been promised he would survive until the 25th of December.

Rocky had done well with his chemo. His hair had started to fall out so Pauline had his head shaved. It always sticks in her mind that she had to pay for this service. It seemed strangely perverse that to lose his hair this way cost money. To begin with, he looked even more ill without hair, but there was something so cheeky and happy about his little face that we almost instantly got used to him being bald.

He had been topped up with blood and had no temperature, so the hospital told us we could go home for Christmas on December 23rd. This was amazing! It seemed that we would have Christmas together at home as a family again. It is impossible for me to really explain what we thought at this time. We were never going to see Christmas as a family again – but now it had all changed. It was great grounds for rejoicing and we thanked God for getting us this far.

I know we had celebrated Christmas once that year, and the girls knew that they were not getting any more presents, but even so, I had quickly been out and bought even more gifts. A number of concerned people who wouldn't normally have done anything also bought the children presents, so we were loaded and ready for another paper-ripping session.

The turkey was in the refrigerator and every bit of Christmas fare was hidden somewhere in the house.

Early on Christmas Eve, I awoke with Pauline next to me; her presence there was becoming a novelty.

Very suddenly around 6am, I made my mind up to go down stairs and put the turkey in the oven. I knew it was not Christmas morning but I felt compelled to act like it was.

Pauline woke as I returned to bed and asked me what I had been doing. I told her that we knew we had today, so we would celebrate Christmas on the 24th and if we had a 25th we would celebrate again. She saw the point and we got into the spirit of the day.

On Thursday 24th December 1998 we had our second Christmas after Rocky's diagnosis. It was wonderful!

After feasting and presents we just enjoyed being together. Again I had neglected to tell the Queen that we were celebrating a day early, so she played no part in the festivities.

When I say that we enjoyed being together, there is of course a caveat. As a family we were under great stress. For Pauline and me, it was difficult to not spend our time looking at Rocky. When we looked at him, it was difficult not to wonder whether we would still have him later in the day. The tension of these times brought headaches, times of frayed tempers and floods of emotion.

It was faith in God and self control that enabled us to enjoy these days. It wasn't to say that we didn't go to sleep some nights wishing that we would wake up to find that it had all been a dream, but we disciplined ourselves to be grateful that we had another day together.

We didn't really expect a "Dallas" experience; you may or may not remember that at one point in the 14 years that the show ran there was a scene with Bobby Ewing in the shower that revealed the previous two seasons of the show to have been a dream!

We had a Christmas Eve service that year and we all gathered in church to celebrate together. As the short meeting came towards an end it was clear that Rocky was starting to spike a temperature. My sister in law said that she would take Pauline and Rocky to Leeds so that I could take the girls to bed.

We had celebrated Christmas, had a great day- even made it to church as a family – but it was time to go back to hospital.

What a great help and support Pauline's sister Lynn and brother in law Dave were at that time. They brought a lot of comfort and tried hard to support us both emotionally and practically.

We were particularly grateful that we had not waited for the 25th to come before we celebrated. Our life at this time helped us to realise the value of spontaneity and the importance of embracing each moment and squeezing the life from it.

Pauline and Rocky arrived on the ward as midnight struck. They were spending Christmas day in hospital after all. Pauline and I were both relieved that we had celebrated on the 24th.

For the girls, the day had been so enjoyable that getting to sleep was no problem. They understood that Christmas had come early for them *twice*, and that the following day we would be going to hospital to visit Rocky *as normal*.

It was now December 25th. We awoke and we had breakfast.

As soon as we could we got over to Jimmy's to see Pauline and Rocky.

Rocky was on intravenous antibiotics to help counter whatever infection was causing his rise in temperature.

The ward was almost empty; about 6 children were there as everyone who wasn't too ill had been sent home.

The first distinctive thing that happened was that the ward had a visit from 'Santa'. Not only did Rocky have a wonderful present, but there was one each for his sisters! Santa was accompanied by a couple of elves that looked remarkably like nurses that we knew. Charge nurse Neil looked wonderful in his pink tutu! I still have the photo and am happy to use it as evidence.

What a fabulous willingness the staff had to entertain the children and make Christmas as special as possible!

The second special thing that happened was the visit to the ward of a star player from the Leeds Rhinos Rugby team. He stood and talked to Rocky, hovering over his bed like an angel from God. We knew nothing to say about the game, but we felt comforted by the fact that God had sent a famous Rugby player to see our little boy.

Lunchtime came and the playroom at the end of the corridor became the parent's canteen. On Sundays and Christmas Day, the Candlelighters charity made sure that parents had a good roast dinner together. We sat there with a traditional Christmas dinner on our knees and talked and laughed with other parents.

Rocky had been befriended by a slightly older boy called Lucas. His brother, Harvey, had leukaemia and was diagnosed within a few days of Rocky. When Harvey didn't want to play, Lucas would come and visit Rocky. They became firm friends and inevitably so did Rocky and Harvey. We sat for lunch that day with their parents, David and Jackie. David had seen Pauline and Lynn arrive with Rocky at midnight. David was very depressed at the thought that they had to be in hospital for Christmas Day, but was comforted when he saw a family arriving at midnight on Christmas Eve who had obviously expected to be at home. It became a talking point with David and the start of many discussions between us.

We had a great time sharing Christmas Dinner that day. The ward was quiet but very special, like the set of some Christmas Hollywood movie. We would have given anything to have not needed to be there, but in reality we had a really good day and were grateful to be together.

Staff went out of their way to make the day as good as possible. What lovely people they were and what great memories we have of the third time we celebrated Christmas that December!

Rocky was tired and weak. I took the girls home because they had lots of energy to play with their many toys. When I rang Pauline that night we said how pleasant Jackie was, but that David was like an old washer-woman. I could talk for England but David put me in the shade. Irrespective of this small fault, we took to them both instantly.

I said to Pauline that maybe whilst on the ward we could share the life we had within us, and perhaps David and Jackie would be our first fruit – we agreed to pray that they would find God.

11 *Counting Calories*

Having a change of lifestyle like this affected everyone's feeding habits.

For Pauline on the ward, the canteen food was terrible. Jacket potatoes with fillings were the nearest to being edible. The steamed puddings were the best thing on the menu, but the novelty soon wore off.

The stress of not being sure of anything from moment to moment wasn't good for the appetite. The constant retching noises and the subsequent collection of vomit to be weighed didn't help. Yes, vomit and diahorrea all had to be collected for weighing. Part of the monitoring of treatment is that every drop in and every drop that came out had to be written down.

For me, comfort eating was good in the evenings after I got home and fed my girls. I went from periods of struggling to eat anything to binging on junk. I was also not "at work" which meant that I had greater access to food and reduced exercise, so I was putting on a few pounds.

Our girls had always been "good eaters", and so fortunately they continued to have a fairly normal diet, except that some of the time eating was rushed because of visitation.

For Rocky however, food was a major issue.

Along with his chemotherapy Rocky was taking a cocktail of anti-emetics to cut nausea.

I still remember him taking Ondansetron, Dexamethasone, and Maxolon. To a great degree these drugs worked from the second cycle of chemo onwards, but chemotherapy didn't exactly make him hungry. Some cancers have steroids as part of the therapy and these children often maintain or increase their weight, but not Rocky.

Our son was a shadow of his former self and his body mass was dangerously low.

Chemotherapy changes the taste buds – bland foods become tasteless and most children lose their interest in sweet things like chocolate, preferring savouries.

His night time feeds through his naso-gastric tube became essential, but encouraging him to take even one extra mouthful of food became a long term project.

To see him naked and count all his bones became a tearful experience.

I became slightly obsessed with feeding him.

So when Rocky said "I think I could eat chicken McNuggets" I was out the door and in the car to the nearest McDonalds without a second thought. When Rocky said "I could eat those little (cherry) tomatoes", I was already on the way to the supermarket. If it was McDonalds, I would go twice a day. For the cherry tomatoes I remember going three times one day (and he ate all 750g).

As much as he had food fads (the tomatoes being the longest lasting), the main problem was the days when he just couldn't face anything, or he did eat and then vomited it all back. He knew that if he didn't eat, he was less likely to vomit; that was a disincentive to eating.

When he discovered that he liked chilli con carne, I became a next generation incarnation of a man called Ironside. I always had a pot of chilli on the stove, and just as the wheelchair bound TV detective was always asking his assistant Mark for a pot of chilli, I was always ready to provide my son with a few mouthfuls.

I can understand why parents would become disenchanted with all the cooking when you attempt to feed a child with cancer, but as far as I was concerned I was happy if my son just ate a mouthful or two – it was better than nothing.

When he was at home Pauline or I would prepare food up to 7 times a day for him, so that we could fight his weight loss.

It isn't something that you normally think about, but food is part of the treatment for childhood cancer. A good diet, and in particular plenty of calories, are an important part of the treatment.

Since these times, the charity Candlelighters has funded two "dinner ladies" on the unit where Rocky was treated. They now provide a kitchen where a lot of children's whims can be catered for at most times of day. This is proving to be a huge success in getting children to eat. In those days, however, if the reheated fish fingers arrived at noon and Rocky wasn't hungry that was the end of it.

To say that weight loss was a problem doesn't really express the fact fully. When first diagnosed Rocky had already lost weight to 23.6kg. By January 1999 Rocky at 4 ½ years old weighed 15kg – no more than a healthy 2 year old and he hovered at that weight for months.

Some parents say that there is too much pressure on parents to deal with the weight issue, but how can there not be? When weight loss is an issue it is inevitable that parents will fight to improve the situation.

The food issue only served to add to the financial pressure that the family was undergoing.

Companies vary in the way they treat their employees at times of family crisis.

I worked for a large multiple retailer who seemed to have no experience of such matters. My immediate line manager was marvellous. He fought hard to keep the company paying me, but very quickly I found myself on statutory sick pay. As a family we were living on the very lowest levels of state benefit. There was no way I could work – or would have wanted to. My family needed me, but the company I worked for didn't understand.

My income had dried up but the cost of living had increased. Not only did we have a family to feed, but we had to maintain daily visits to Leeds and provide separate food for Pauline on the ward.

There were extra pairs of pyjamas to buy and various other items that made life comfortable on a hospital ward.

Rocky had qualified for Disability Living Allowance and there were one or two charity grants to assist towards the costs we had of looking after him when he was at home – extra bedding and clothes, etc.

The cost of keeping our car on the road was increasing and all the time there were unanticipated costs. There were also those presents that I couldn't resist buying for my son. We went from being in control of our finances to having no control at all.

To complicate matters, my employers were awkward to the point of persecuting me.

Not once, but twice, they accidentally paid me my salary. This doesn't sound bad until you realise that whilst in the hospital with Rocky they rang me each time to demand that I repaid the error THAT DAY in person to my line manager.

So on two occasions I had to leave my little boy to drive back to York and pay my manager a cheque the same day I received it. It was not acceptable for me to stick it through the letterbox on the way home or pay the next day. Yet none of this was my mistake!

The benefits agency began to pursue me for fraud. I claimed that I was not receiving a salary (which was true) but when they wrote to my employer they were told that I was in receipt of full pay. It is difficult to get the benefits agency on your side when your employer calls you a liar!

The stress of having no money, being accused of benefit fraud and occasionally being paid by mistake was starting to show. Pauline used to say to me that money didn't matter when your son was sick, and she was right, but it was all extra pressure at a time when we didn't need it.

On top of all this my employer wrote to me demanding that I attend a medical exam. I was on sick leave due to "family stress" which is what GP's put on a sick note in times like these. It was quite clear that I was well (?) and that it was my son that was ill, but I was still asked to attend a medical. This was of course a process that they were going through in order to dismiss me, and they clearly hoped that they could get rid of me.

I kept in touch with my line manager who occasionally shed a tear with me and was clearly a man of great emotion. I really appreciated him, and he was infuriated with the way I was treated.

After a few months, he rang me to tell me that I would be receiving a letter telling me that I would not be terminated but that I would remain on statutory sick pay and could return to the company at any time in the next 18 months, with my salary and rank intact.

The letter did indeed arrive – which totally revolutionised life for us.

To obtain this letter, my manager Dave had met up with a company director and bought him enough to drink so that he could be persuaded to sign the letter confirming my status.

Despite the method used to obtain this protection, I was very grateful! I thanked Dave for his ingenuity and I thanked God for answering prayer.

While Rocky was subject to a cocktail of drugs, we were subject to a cocktail of pressures.

Even though this matter was resolved, we were clearly getting behind financially and were to finish treatment with a certain amount of debt.

Many of the parents we met on Ward 10 were to separate and divorce during or immediately after treatment. The pressures of being apart, the stress and fear faced daily, and the constant financial pressures all contributed.

Pauline and I were so blessed to be together.

12 *Cycles & Tests*

I have discovered that, in life, most people like to find a pattern. Children are most comfortable with a routine and so are most adults. When change enters someone's life, there tends to be a searching for the hidden "why?" It is not surprising that most parents who have a child with cancer ask the question, "how did my child develop this cancer – where did it come from?"

Unfortunately there is often no way of answering that question. I have spoken to parents who have tried to investigate the existence of clusters of cases, the proximity of power stations and family medical histories to try and get an answer. In fact, the clinicians and researchers are also asking these questions, with money constantly being poured into the gathering of all such data.

One simplistic answer that is often given today is that many childhood cancers seem to be triggered by simple viruses. A child catches a virus which has a totally unexpected outcome because a process that is abnormal starts within the body. One assumes this has something to do with a genetic predisposition, but the matter is far from clear. There are now genes that have been identified that have a statistical link with cancers, but even these do not seem to guarantee an outcome.

As part of a trial, Rocky was tested for a particular gene that suspicions had been levelled at. It was supposed that the presence of this gene might make a successful outcome of the treatment less likely. The science was unclear on the issue and so when we asked

Rocky's consultant what the result was she declined to answer. This made us think that the result was bad, but her response was that we had to proceed with treatment and whatever this indicator meant (which wasn't clear) they were going to throw everything at the cancer.

Just knowing that this information was out there was something we were uncomfortable with, but years later we had a conversation with her again on this issue and she told us that the test had been negative. She confirmed that at the time they had not known the outcome of the research, but that today they knew that the relapse rate of children with the gene was much higher.

We hadn't lived near Sellafield and had no known family history problems, so there was no pattern we could see, but to be fair, we were not looking for a natural pattern. We saw all that was going on as a result of a spiritual condition that had its roots in the garden of Eden. The Bible teaches that, in the beginning, man rebelled against God and that as a result, sin, sickness, corruption and death had been released into our world. Surely the gene pool was getting worse the farther we were away from Eden. This backlash in Rocky's body was not God's plan, but instead it was the result of the chaos that we ourselves had released on Earth.

Some would say that this was religious gibberish, but this is what the Bible says and what we believe as a family. Therefore we were not focussing on a natural cause but praying for a supernatural solution.

As much as we had been led to believe we wouldn't all see December 25th 1998, we were well into the New Year and Rocky was still fighting. We knew there were no certainties from day to day, but we also recognised that somewhere along the line the prayers that were going up were helping.

I had developed an email list that I used to send an update out once a week or more often if I felt necessary. It enabled me to disseminate news and prayer requests quickly, without having to repeat myself to many people over the phone.

We were spending most of our time nursing our immunosuppressed son, with no certainty that he couldn't die within the day. There were no certainties, except our belief that God loved us. There were no patterns that we could see had brought us here and our lives were continually dominated by change. Yet in all of what was going on, a new structure or pattern of life was established by the cycles of treatment.

The new pattern of life went something like this: hydration, chemo, three days in hospital, a day or two at home, infection, five days in hospital on antibiotics just in time to start the ten day cycle again.

However, just when you thought you had a pattern, it was time for the testing regime to start.

After four cycles of chemo would come a liver function test, kidney function, heart, hearing, CT scan, bone scan, traffines from the hip bone and fluid from the spinal column. It then took a week or so to get all this information processed before the cycle could restart.

The problem was the toxicity and high dose of the treatment. If they gave Rocky any less treatment, the cancer would not be affected; if they gave him any more treatment he might have multiple organ failure which would also kill him. Whereas the effect on the kidneys and liver were the most common, deafness, sterility and damage to other organs were sometimes a result also.

The other test that Rocky had after each four cycles was an unusual one. This test revealed the amount of activity in his skeleton, but it was also therapeutic. Before injection, the MIBG (Meta-Iodo-Benzyl-Guanidine) is attached to a form of iodine that is radioactive. The MIBG chemical is taken up by the neuroblastoma cells. Scans then look for the uptake of radioactivity in the body, revealing where the neuroblastoma cells are. This is a very sensitive and accurate method. In addition, because the radiation is taken up by the cancer it can become a form of localised radiotherapy and so might have the beneficial side effect of killing cancer cells.

Rocky was given a high dose of iodine before the test because the thyroid naturally takes up iodine and it was important to make sure that the gland did not absorb the radioactive type.

For his MIBG, Rocky had to be transferred to another hospital and the radioactive isotope had to be flown in from Holland and brought by motorcycle courier to the hospital. This was one of those tests that reminded me what good value the National Health Service is!

After these tests, Rocky's urine was radioactive and too much cuddling wasn't advised. He had to be kept away from pregnant women and we had to wear rubber gloves and disposable aprons to look after him. We joked with him that he was 'radioactive boy' and he joked that he might have some adventures like Peter Parker (Spider-Man, who in comic-book-land was bitten by a radioactive spider).

When it came to bone scans, CT scans and MIBG scans, many children Rocky's age had to be sedated. Rocky was amazing at lying still when you told him to, and so he stayed awake through them all. This isn't to say he didn't flinch occasionally, but in the main he could lie still for 30 minutes at a time. When he got off the machine, he would run around the room happily!

The test week that occurred after four cycles of chemo was quite stressful because there was the associated wait for results. With the MIBG scan, we could see the picture being built up as scintillations were detected and shown as little red dots. The question was always, what did they mean? What was normal and what was not? Waiting to get results caused a suspension in treatment and the ever present question "what if the treatment has stopped working?"

There was the potential (because we heard it happen to other parents) that we would be taken on one side to be told that the treatment was ineffective and that it was time to put Rocky in a hospice to die. It was also possible that we would be told the treatment was killing him and that they would not be able to continue it for that reason. The message we wanted to hear was that the cancer had all gone away and that Rocky was going to grow up, have his own children and live a full life.

There is something comforting in the predictability of life. Having a child with cancer totally removed that comforting predictability. Even the repetition of cycles of chemotherapy might be described as giving a framework for your life, except that they were not that straightforward. Infections and tests broke up the pattern of treatment. The pressure of knowing that the next cycle might be so toxic that it could bring death also took away any comfort from the repetitive nature of the treatment.

It is almost impossible to express the relationship you have with chemotherapy as a parent. When emotionally detached it is just medicine. When it is your son having the toxic soup pumped into his chest on one level you can welcome a treatment that may save your child, but on another you dread its side effects and its potential to kill.

After the first round of testing, it was good news. The cancer in Rocky's skeleton was reducing and he was well enough to continue the treatment for another 4 cycles. How bizarre it was that we were pleased to be having another round of chemo.

13 *Accentuating the Positive*

Pain, death and suffering.

Pressure, anxiety and panic.

Tears, fears and insomnia.

These words and others describe the environment we lived in and the feelings that surrounded us.

It is possible to move into a dirty and run down house on a poor estate and make a good home there. It takes hard work and commitment – it also requires that you look towards the desired outcome and not the surroundings.

We worked hard to not be changed by our environment, but instead to create a new one that we were the major influence in. This is not to say that others weren't trying. The professionals we had continuous contact with were marvellous, but whatever impact others have, ultimately we are the ones that make it work.

At times my mind would go back to "The Hiding Place" – the story of Corrie ten Boom. She survived the horrors of the concentration camp in the Second World War, waiting for freedom to come, but facing the fact that death was hovering nearby. Just like in Corrie's story, God was also hovering nearby and daily we chose to fix our attention on Him rather than on the proximity of death.

It was as if the air was thick with infection. We lived in an environment dominated by a miasma and it was up to us to blow it away. Next to St James' hospital is the excellent Thackeray

Museum. In there, a display of old Leeds shows the way infection used to spread and the realistic smells make a visit before lunch preferable to one with a full stomach. Wind blows from high pressure to low. We were a family under pressure, but instead of yielding to it, we had to harness it so that something fresh blew all around us.

We have three words; breath, wind and spirit. The New Testament has one word for all three. To a Greek speaking person, the translation of their one word into breath, wind or spirit is contextual. In the context we found ourselves, the wind we needed was really the Spirit of God. We prayed and prayed for our son's healing. We also prayed that the Spirit of God would blow out of us, changing the environment around us and bringing something fresh to all that we met.

A change like this does not happen because of personality or predisposition. It happens because of the choice to involve the Spirit of God in our lives. Many days it was a fight to find the positives and be grateful for even little things, but I came to the point that every day in which I still had my son there was a reason to whoop and holler. We laughed a lot on the ward. We laughed when nose tubes came out in the vomit bowl, we laughed when a poo was 'sharp' and hurt Rocky on the way out. We laughed at little things that he found amusing and there was a whole lot of cuddling.

At that time legislation hadn't been brought in banning smoking in public buildings. Some nights Pauline would sit in a confined space with other mums as they smoked and she would bring a breath of fresh air to them in response to their questions about what was different about her. Other times a nurse would come into to spend a minute with her and Rocky, just because they had been under stress with another family and needed somewhere to recover; and a gentle breeze would blow.

Other professionals visiting the ward would leave us until last, so that whatever they had just faced in another bay, they would find something a little more refreshing with the Redmans.

We never forced our views on anyone but many asked what it was about us, and what we believed. As a result we were able to talk about the goodness of God on that ward many times.

Our friendship grew with David and Jackie. He was a man who couldn't go 15 yards to the kitchen to make a cup of tea and get back in less than an hour. Many times we sent out search parties for him! He loved having deep and meaningful conversations and if there was someone in the corridor he wouldn't pass without engaging them. We shared many "deep and meaningful" talks and as a family we were delighted when they found Christ for themselves and got stuck into church.

A wind had blown and something refreshing had happened. By the end of March we had received the answer to our Christmas Day prayer.

We found that our hearts went out to other couples and their children. We even found that our hearts went out to the staff. This wasn't just about us. We had the opportunity to influence others in a positive way and stimulate them as people of hope.

The couple who went home every night and left their little boy on the ward alone saddened me. Rocky noticed. I think he was relieved that we never left him; we made sure he was never in any doubt that we weren't going home without him.

When a child died, the atmosphere on the ward would be terrible. Even today I can still sense it when I walk onto the unit. Any little hope that people had would be dashed. I remember the day that the couple who were always arguing were bereaved. They fought all the time, but one day after their rowing their little boy started to change colour. Before he died he was green – 'Incredible Hulk' green. It was very dark on the ward that day. It happened so quickly, they were whisked away. We mourned with them, but for the sake of our boy we prayed hard and worked hard to turn it around.

Another boy was lost, but hope wasn't. We were still hanging on, and blowing hard.

It wasn't all altruistic either – we needed to keep our focus for Rocky's benefit.

Remember the boy whose eye had been hanging out when I first arrived at the ward?

His tumour went down with chemotherapy and his face and eye went back to normal. He and Rocky became firm friends even though he was a few years older. His mum came to see him once a week. When in hospital he spent most of the time without a parent, and when he had to go to clinic he would catch a bus across Leeds by himself to get there. Besides the fact that we just wanted to take him home with us, situations like that made us realise how blessed we were.

It is sad when any child gets cancer. It is particularly sad when there is one solitary parent to care with no family support. The burden on one carer is enormous, but they do it all for love.

It is worst of all when the child appears to have no one who is able to give consistent care. Some parents struggle with their emotions so much that they don't know how to help their own child; others become debilitated by their shock and fear. In some of these cases there are parents who simply don't know how to show that they care. Sometimes a child was clearly "at risk" before cancer.

I am convinced that God himself draws close to those little ones.

One day when Rocky was going to clinic, we realised we hadn't seen his friend who used to come alone on the bus for a couple of weeks. He had died suddenly. I remember seeing the loss on Rocky's face and hearing him say that he would pray about it.

I so wish we could have taken that little boy home.

14 *Ad Nauseam*

The cycles of chemo progressed and Rocky became very tolerant of the treatment. On average St James treat two neuroblastoma cases per year. In 1998-99 they had two boys who were both admitted within a week of each other and went through the treatment in a parallel fashion.

The other little boy lives quite near us today and is one of the elite club of survivors. During treatment, however, he was very intolerant of the chemo and ended up in intensive care a few times. No-one would have believed he would have survived the course, but we thank God that he did.

To relate the monotony of the same four cycles of chemo and the testing regime over and over might switch you off the story, so for the sake of avoiding too much detail about life with a handy sick-bowl let me now skip over some parts of our story.

Very quickly, you adjust to your son being the centre of attention – even if it is in a negative way.

I remember a man storming towards me out of his car when we parked outside Pizza Hut in a disabled bay. He laced into me about the misuse of the bay as I unloaded Rocky's wheelchair and gently lifted him into it. Without another word the man apologised and backed away sheepishly realising that checking for a disabled badge and looking beyond the adults in a car would both be good things to do in future.

On another occasion in a supermarket a parent stood by whilst her little boy tried to pull the NG tube out of Rocky's nose.

Another time a young girl came up to Rocky and asked him why he was bald! I can still see the smile on his face as, with his head on one side, he said to her "because I have cancer". To be fair, so many little boys had their hair cut short either because of fashion or because of head lice that baldness didn't set Rocky apart too much – it was the tube hanging out of his nose and the wheelchair that gave him away.

To try and help Pauline's tiredness from not sleeping in hospital, I volunteered to swap with her and stay with Rocky for a week so that she could go home with the girls and get some rest at nights. I bought new pyjamas and stopped on the ward experiencing for myself what those nights are like. I became the one who got the late night call from home, and the one to experience the delight of the Z-bed.

The ward has junior doctors on rotation as part of the team and every six months they changed. This rotation had just happened. One morning as I got up to go to the bathroom a junior doctor saw me and commented how much he liked my pyjamas. A male nurse stood behind him gave me a big wink and I was definitely spooked by the experience. This became something Pauline and I joked about and every time I have ever put on a pair of PJ's for the first time Pauline has told me how much she likes them and winked.

Ten years later, I was visiting the ward on a day in which some staff were wearing pyjamas for charity. The same charge nurse that had been on duty that morning years before came up to me and said that he had expected me to be wearing PJ's as he knew I had some nice ones – he gave me another big wink! It took me a minute to realise that he was referring to the events of a decade before – and then I laughed and laughed that he should have remembered my sensitive moment!

Pauline couldn't stand not being with Rocky. She loved her own bed, but at her insistence I think I only stopped on the ward

5 nights and then she was back with our boy. I loved being with Rocky, but knowing that she needed to be there was enough for me. I also didn't have to worry about a certain doctor and his interest in my pyjamas!

Our children were a great joy to us and they loved family life. It was therefore natural for us to imagine a day in which our children would themselves have their own families. Except, would Rocky? The treatment would often result in sterility. When I look back at the email I sent out I would sometimes mention this under points for prayer. On one occasion I asked our friends to pray for *correct function in his heart liver, kidney, pancreas, hearing or eyesight AND that he will not be sterile*! What a bizarre disease where the only treatment risks damaging all your key organs and your ability to reproduce.

In Star Trek 4 'The Voyage Home' the crew go back in time to 20th century earth to save the whales. On visiting a hospital Dr McCoy overhears doctors discussing a patient's course of chemotherapy and refers to it as sounding like "the Spanish Inquisition". I can't help but wonder if one day man will have advanced enough to deal with neuroblastoma with a simple pill like McCoy would have prescribed.

Today we look back at some treatments – like the Nobel Prize winning lobotomy – and consider it barbaric. Perhaps we will still advance, but if we do it will be thanks to charities like Candlelighters who invest in research and the great sharing of data between agencies all across the world from trials. This aside, I can say that the future sterility of a five year old boy was of great concern to us.

In the same email I mention that "Pauline is doing well. I am proud of the impact she is having on other lives. She is surrounded by death and the dying, and yet is full of hope for our boy. She spends almost as much time helping others in the hospital as she does looking after Rocky." My perception of her then was very much what it is now – pride. All through this episode and since she has acquitted herself well, and most importantly has always been there for the family, but not exclusively – she has been there for others too.

One night I rang her at bed time to get the story of a woman she had befriended on the ward. Her 17 year old son had come in for an amputation because of cancer in his leg. She had lost his brother the year before when he was 17 in a vehicle accident. His older brother was dying from MS and his sister was blind. This woman was living with a whole different level of trouble. Religious talk wouldn't help this woman, but Pauline communicating the hope that was in her could. This lady was like many who crossed our paths – in touch for a while and then not. I think the brevity of contact that we have with people is one of the reasons that the New Testament says "*Always be prepared to give an answer to everyone who asks you to give the reason for the hope that you have*" (1 Peter 3:15 NIV).

15 *Little Miracles*

When fighting cancer other answers to prayer could seem trivial, but each 'little miracle' we had was an encouragement to fight on for the greater goal.

We had decided that whereas the financial issues were very real, we would not allow anything to come between us and our boy. Even if at the end of treatment we had to sell our house or go bankrupt, we would do what was necessary to keep our family together – the rest was just 'stuff'.

One little miracle was to do with UVPC. We had to replace the window in Rocky's bedroom. It was the coldest room in the house, and we needed to make sure we were keeping him at a good temperature. I ordered a double glazed window for £698. (The price is correct to the nearest I can remember – this will be important soon!)

There was about 6 weeks lead time on the window, but the day was coming when I would have to pay on fitting. It was a Sunday and the window was being fitted the following day. We had nothing in the bank at all. I didn't tell anyone about the need and I certainly didn't tell anyone what the bill was.

A friend came up to me at church and said that God had spoken to him and told him to give me some money. He said it was a very specific amount and that God had told him I would understand what it was for. I thanked him and put the envelope in my pocket without opening it. I expected £20.

When I got home there was £698.50 in the envelope. I marvelled at the bounty! I could pay in full for the window the following day – but why 50p more than I needed?

So I rang my friend and told him that I had opened the envelope. I also told him that I needed the money for this window and that I had to pay the next day. I thanked him for listening to God and being so generous. I hesitated but asked him – why the 50p? He told me that he had been near me in church when one of the girls had come up to me and asked for 50p to get a can of cola from the machine. I had responded "I am sorry darling – daddy doesn't even have 50p". When he had got home he prayed about giving us some money and God said £698 – but he added the 50p so that next time I was asked for a can I would have the money!

What a wonderful miracle!

As you can imagine, I was prepared next time we went to church and I bought that can of coke.

We also paid for the window in full and Rocky's room became a lot warmer place to be in.

A little while later we started to have car troubles. We had a couple of sensor faults on our Mitsubishi Space Wagon – a seven-seater car that held the six of us and Rocky's wheelchair comfortably. It was seven years old and had been a great blessing. We had a couple of £200 bills which were very difficult to pay at this time, but God helped us. The real shock came when we broke down, had to be towed and the garage rang up saying that it would be around £2500 to repair!

The blow that this was to us was hard to describe. No car that we would all fit in! No income and no way of replacing the car! This was just the sort of problem that we didn't need!

I told the garage that I couldn't afford it and explained our situation. In an instant the manager told me that I was eligible for a free vehicle. Because Rocky was receiving Disability Living Allowance – a state benefit that helped with the care that he needed, we were also eligible for a 'motability' vehicle. A week later we had a brand new Space Wagon on the drive.

This meant that we no longer owned our family car – but at least we had one and all it cost us was the fuel we used. This certainly felt like another miracle.

Some days the answers to prayer were less obvious. Out of the blue a parcel arrived from some children in a school in Texas. It contained pictures and letters that they had made to encourage Rocky and us too. People that we didn't know and hadn't realised we had any connection with were praying for us.

An envelope through the door, an anonymous gift, a cheque from a friend; many little gifts came when we needed them most. We never missed a mortgage payment and we paid every bill on time. Little miracles they were, but miracles all the same.

16 *Who Knows?*

Rocky's fifth birthday, 8th May 1999, was spent in hospital. The staff organised food and a party with a disco. They bought him presents and his sisters loved being there and dancing. This week was the only time we can remember him sitting on his bed crying for us to take him home. Three times in a couple of days he went through this. Then fortunately his temperature and counts were stable and we were able to go back home.

Rocky's party wasn't the only social event on the ward. Once a month there was 'karaoke night'. This was a firm favourite with parent and child alike. Elizabeth, Melody and Arielle all loved a microphone in their hand. In fact at one stage Libby got through rather a lot of toy microphones due to over use, so I started making them out of a bundle of straws with a cap of tinfoil on the top. Pauline would get other parents to join in too. On one occasion we came through for the karaoke even though Rocky wasn't in hospital just because the girls were looking forward to it so much!

The great highlight of every week was the "Jolly Trolley". Jolly was the nickname for Sandra who had worked on the ward for many years. She had contacts with people who donated all sorts of sweets for the children. As a treat, children would get the opportunity to be Jolly's helper and go around pushing the trolley with her as she gave out a bag of all their favourite jellies and chews. I can remember how Rocky looked forward to it being his turn, and I can still not get over the ingenuity and compassion of the care worker who thought of this wonderful idea.

The next year Pauline nominated Sandra to BBC Look North as a millennium champion for her work in this way. We were overjoyed when she won 'Hero of the year' and Pauline had to be on the TV to be interviewed with Harry Gration and Clare Frisby as Jolly was presented with her award. This award was used to draw attention to the great work performed by all the staff on the children's and teen-age cancer unit at St James.

After the fourth cycle of chemotherapy tests showed that the rate of cancer in Rocky's skeleton was diminishing, so treatment would continue. After the eighth cycle, tests showed that the cancer had been eradicated from all parts of the skeleton except the hips and the knees. Disappointingly, after the twelfth cycle, the scans still showed activity in a hot spot in his hip.

When the idea of treatment had first been broached, the consultant had said it was possible to have up to sixteen cycles of chemo and so we were ready for another four. It was two days after his birthday that I asked her what came next. I was taken aback when she said "I don't know". I was not of the age that thinks of consultants as gods, nor was I so out of touch with God that I could get Him mixed up; however, I had come to believe that she knew what she was doing, so it was more than slightly unsettling to hear that she didn't. Having said that, I admired her honesty and preferred it to any alternative.

A few things became clear; sixteen cycles were possible in theory, but they weren't aware that any more than twelve had actually ever been given in a case like this. Although Rocky's kidney function test had come back better after the twelfth cycle than the eighth, there was a general belief that he would not tolerate another four cycles without severe organ damage somewhere. There was also the law of diminishing returns – that if twelve cycles hadn't got the cancer out of his hip, perhaps sixteen wouldn't either. Then the torment that he would have been put through would have been for no benefit.

We had expected a stem cell replacement to be the next step if he was clear. This is like a bone marrow replacement but instead of collecting bone marrow cells from a donor, the patient's own cells are used. This treatment was now not on the agenda, because Rocky was not clear of cancer.

I decided that it didn't matter that she didn't know what to do, because God did. So I let her know that I would be getting people to pray that she would find out what to do and know how to continue. She genuinely thanked me for this.

Trephines had been taken from Rocky. This test involved the removal of pieces of bone from the hip which had to be decalcified and then examined. This process took three weeks from collection to report. This was the only test that we hadn't had the results back from.

As we prayed there were still the questions. What if we have come this far and they can't stop the cancer? What if all we can do now is slip backwards into the despond of disease and certain death?

To have come so far….

We prayed, our friends prayed, and then the answer came.

The consultant rang us up. We were at home and it was a warm sunny afternoon. She started the call with the words "I now know what to do". I thanked God – because whatever she was going to say next, this was the very thing we had prayed for.

The bone samples had come back riddled with cancer cells but every one of them was dead!

The consultant was happy that the treatment had been very effective in the hip and that a two pronged strategy would kill anything remaining. The next step would be to proceed with the stem cell replacement. This began with a final chemo which itself might knock out any remaining rogue cells. Immediately afterwards Rocky would undergo 20 shots of radio therapy into the point on his hip that had showed up on the scan. This might result in uneven growth in his hip in the future but would probably not disable him in any way. It was very likely that radiotherapy would eradicate any remaining live cancer cells.

The consultant was happy to proceed and so were we.

That waiting time was over.

17 *Melphalan*

It was at the end of May 1999 that Arielle's long awaited turn for an NHS tonsillectomy came along. The bizarre thing was that Pauline had to be in St James in Leeds with Rocky, whilst I had to stop overnight in York District with Arielle.

Seeing her brother's bravery helped Arielle a lot, but our own carefree attitude about "it's only a tonsillectomy" also settled her. The difference between the provision on the ward and the care given between the two was unbelievable. The difference that charitable contributions from Candlelighters make to the care and provision for children with cancer is enormous!

There were still four children to a bay and four z-beds for parents to stay on, but that is where the comparison ended. I was of course the only dad there – this was looked upon with some suspicion. The shock to the system, though, was the other three parents gathered in a corner crying together about their children's impending operations. Here we had a routine procedure with the smallest of risk and 23 miles away a ward full of children who were just fighting for life. The contrast was stark and I struggled with it. I had to remind myself that no one likes their child to have surgery.

By 8.30am the following morning Arielle was discharged, home and biking around the street. She had a very good attitude about recovery.

Stem cell replacement wasn't such a routine process as a tonsillectomy. The start of Rocky's stem cell replacement was to stimulate his body to produce them chemically. Every day he had to have injections of a drug to facilitate this. When we were at home, a district nurse came to do this. The drug could not go into his Hickman line, but had to be injected into muscle, so Rocky went ballistic every time she arrived. He still didn't like needles. I am sure they hurt too, but with some coaxing from Melody and a lot of cuddles he reluctantly had each one. Of all his treatment I think this was what he resisted the most.

When your child desperately doesn't want an injection and you love your child so much, it is very hard to force the process, or even observe it. Just as discipline only really works when motivated by love, that same love helps you do what is necessary. After a week of injections, we were just as relieved as Rocky was that they were over. Then he had to have a catheter fitted into the top of his chest, just below his neck. This procedure gave a place from which stem cells could be collected. On the Friday 11th June 1999 he had the operation to fit the catheter and on the following Monday the collection began.

Rocky had to go to the clinic and lay on a bed whilst a machine took his blood out, filtered it for stem cells through a selective centrifuge and replaced it back into his body. The process lasted a few hours and usually required a couple of sessions. After one session they told us that they had harvested enough cells. In fact, his count was the second highest in the records of the blood transfusion service and therefore only required the one session. The "vascath" could be removed from his neck and the procedure could really start.

So Rocky and mum got a side room on Ward 10, for one of the few times ever. The process was explained to us in full and an excellent charge nurse, whose caring nature and skill could not be disputed, sat us down. He began by saying how partic-ularly well Rocky had tolerated the twelve cycles of chemo and that he had not experienced any adverse reactions or any extreme pain. He told us that this was about to change.

The first stage was to be hydrated and then given the final chemotherapy – Melphalan. The high toxicity of the Melphalan would hopefully complete the job in his hip, but it would effectively remove all of Rocky's own bone marrow, killing the good and the bad cells together.

The severity of this chemo could not be understated and it would put Rocky in a weaker state than he had experienced thus far. The nurse was quick to point out that the main side effect is the ulceration of the digestive tract from the mouth all the way to the anus. As Rocky would not be able to eat throughout this period, he would be fed by TPN (Total Parenteral Nutrition). This would go through his Hickman line every day and would be a mixture of all the key essentials of digested food that were in a solution suitable for being added directly to the bloodstream.

Because of the severity of the treatment and the total loss of immunity that Rocky would experience, it would be a time in which infections would be of the highest level of risk.

The key point of this discussion was that we needed to prepare for the pain that Rocky would go through and be ready to prompt the staff for pain relief medication. In particular, the nurse stressed to me that Rocky would need oral morphine straight away and very quickly would need it intravenously.

I remember taking him to task about this and saying that he shouldn't paint the picture too black, because Rocky would surprise him through this too. I told him that I didn't believe Rocky would need I.V. morphine. This became a bit of a polite spat, but I felt that he was trying to undermine our hope – something which he had no right to do.

Pauline summarised it by saying to him 'Don't you think your patients need to hear words of hope instead of all this negativity?'

Hydration by drip took 24 hours.

Melphalan was one injection into his line and took 15 minutes in total. It was so hard to believe that one small dose could be so unbelievably toxic.

Very quickly, Rocky began to vomit a lot and he appeared to have had the stuffing knocked out of him. He was weak and listless – just lying there in bed.

When they brought his stem cells back to pump into him the room had a strong smell of sweetcorn – this was because of the liquid holding the cells. The process of gathering the cells had taken ages, but in 30 minutes they were all back inside him.

Within a few days he couldn't swallow water and anything that we tried to get down him came straight back up. As predicted his mouth became sore and ulcerated – evidence that this was happening throughout his gut.

He would vomit phlegm and pass blood. However, Rocky's pain was in control but he looked sick and uncomfortable. He began to take some oral morphine but he never needed to take I.V. pain relief.

During a period of about 6 weeks Pauline didn't leave Rocky alone in their room. The vomiting and diarrhoea continued and very rarely did Pauline get more than an hour's uninterrupted sleep. My beautiful blonde was turning into a zombie – but a zombie who loved her son and was doing the best for him!

During this time they made a CT map of his pelvis so that the radiographers could plan exactly where to direct the next stage of treatment. We were also advised of the possibility of taking part in a trial of another drug to help stimulate the immune system. This trial was about to close and it would be touch and go to be part of it. We really wanted this for Rocky. To qualify, his blood counts would have to achieve a certain level within 40 days of completing the stem cell therapy.

At the start of this process the negative charge nurse had a couple of days off work with an eye infection.

When he returned he was visibly surprised to see how well Rocky was. As charmingly as possible, I expressed my surprise that he was back at work so quickly "I expected you to be on a morphine infusion by now," I said. He replied "Well, we can all be wrong sometimes, can't we?" Our little banter revealed a mutual understanding that Rocky hadn't reacted as badly as had been expected to the treatment.

It has to be said, though, that this was indeed his lowest time on treatment and it must be underlined just how dangerous this procedure is.

After all this banter, I still see that nurse today and I am proud to know him, as he is a true professional.

On July 5th I wrote this to my email list:

Rocky has clearly turned the corner in respect of the current treatment. His blood counts are unstable, but showing an upward trend in the all important neutrophil (immunity). He is having platelets tonight and the consultant is very pleased with him. He is talking again, although his mouth has a number of purple blood blisters (especially his tongue and lips) and he is still bleeding a bit. He was well enough to go to Cookridge hospital to have his assessment for radiotherapy. They intend to start on 21st July daily for 4 weeks. It is the crest of his right hip that they are targeting.

Pauline has had a hard day. I should have been there but didn't think it through. The consultant was not used to children and had an unpleasant manner (the staff on Ward 10 know him!) He made some wide ranging statements which were upsetting, until they were explained later by the nurses.

Rocky has been tattooed (literally) where the rays have to go in – these are permanent tattoos although not large. None of them say "Manchester United" or "Kiss me" – they are just x marks the spot! They say the growth of his right hip will be significantly affected. The consultant basically thought this wasn't an issue as we were lucky he was alive!!!

The tattooing seemed a little shocking, but it is essential that they have fixed points that cannot move to line his body up before firing the radioactive particles.

My boy's bone marrow was being renewed from within. In some weird parallel my spirit was being renewed within me.

18 *Total Eclipse*

From being a child I had looked up at the stars. My knowledge of astronomy had meant that, from being a boy, I had known that the first real opportunity I would have to see a total eclipse of the sun from the UK would be on August 11th 1999. It seems strange to wait for something for 30 years, but then some Bible characters waited even longer for God's promise to come to pass.

The last nine months had felt longer than the thirty year wait for an eclipse. They were also a little more significant to me.

Rocky's counts finally came up enough for us to take him out of hospital for the day on 19th July – Pauline's birthday.

The 21st of August was to be a very significant day. Radiotherapy was to start this day, but more importantly for Rocky, the new Star Wars Movie (Episode 1:The Phantom Menace) was out and we had tickets to see it.

From being a weak frail little boy who could barely get off the bed a week before, he was so excited about seeing the first Star Wars movie of his generation that he couldn't wait to get out.

We went for our first shot of radiotherapy.

Many very ill and elderly people were queuing to receive their doses. For children a timed appointment was given where we could avoid the queue and the unpleasantness of what could be seen. We walked in through an entrance that avoided the queue and straight in for his shot.

The high tech particle beams of Cookridge hospital were nothing compared to the blasters and lightsabers found in a galaxy far, far away…

It was as if George Lucas had written a new movie especially for my son. Rocky loved the pod racing, the space ships and the light sabre fights. After being so inactive he seemed to use more adrenaline and excitement than any little boy should have at his disposal. When the movie was over he was certainly ready to sleep.

At that time, we still had to go to the clinic every day for blood tests and we were fighting to qualify for the interluken trial. We wanted to be part of this trial because of the benefit to Rocky's immune system. Unfortunately, we discovered that we had missed it and there was no way we could be included. This came as a blow.

The same day that we found this out we also discovered that a little boy with whose mum Pauline had become friendly had relapsed. Harry had also been treated for neuroblastoma and a lump had appeared on his neck. Their fear was palpable. This was horrendous news.

We drew as close to this family as we could and we organised prayer. This little boy was given a couple of weeks to live.

Meanwhile we were still making the daily trips to Leeds for Radiotherapy.

So it was on August 11th that we were driving back as the eclipse approached almost totality. The sky darkened and the event I had looked forward to for thirty years was happening. We pulled into the side of the road and used the protective glasses that we had been issued with to watch the sun as the moon ate it away before our very eyes.

To Rocky this was just another thrill, to me it was the completion of a boyhood dream. However with the darkening of our personal skies and the once in a life time experience of childhood cancer, the event was somehow an anticlimax.

The eclipse didn't reach absolute totality from Leeds, but it was as near as could be. For everyone it was darker all around, but it would pass and the light would return. We had been to a dark place for many months, but the light had filled our hearts and now we could see the brightness breaking through.

As totality passed, Rocky and I got back in the car and completed the journey home to Pauline and his sisters. Our darkness was passing, but for others around us it was only getting worse.

On August 17th 1999 Rocky's formal treatment for cancer came to an end with his last shot of radiotherapy. Our little boy experienced some redness and soreness in the skin, but otherwise he tolerated it brilliantly.

Our friends nearby in York were watching their little boy get worse as death approached. He was on a lot of morphine. We were watching the first signs of fuzz re-growing on Rocky's head. 'Hair for Christmas', I declared.

Very soon after we were able to enjoy a Candlelighters break at Bridlington. The log cabins are fitted out very well and it was amazing how much we could enjoy this simple seaside resort. Rocky had a great time and so did his sisters. It was great to be away as a family. There was still a line in his chest and our boy was very underweight but it actually seemed as if we were going to enjoy some good times together now.

Whilst at Bridlington we visited the John Bull Rock factory which makes a wide range of confectionary and have an excellent factory tour. Rocky absolutely loved the place and had a great time making his own lollipop out of chocolate. There was a competition for children and Rocky won a huge hamper of John Bull confectionary. He and his sisters were very grateful indeed!

My memory of riding a swing as a child is fading somewhat, but as I remember, the highs are more fun than the lows, but the sheer speed of the experience is what adds the excitement. We were not on swings or roundabouts, and we weren't playing, but there was a rapid movement of events in our lives coupled with highs and lows. Only our prayer lives and faith in God kept us from losing our balance and falling off.

When you are practicing being grateful, a box of sweet rock is a huge blessing; we banked it as another great memory, but our thoughts were never very far from the parents with the dying child to whom we were linked by disease.

Christmas 1997
- unaware of what was to come

Rocky held by his sisters
only 1 day old
(May 1994)

Below: Normal, healthy, curious little boy

Right: Christmas celebrated December 6th 1998 with Big-Bear

Photos during treatment, May/June 1999
The treatment was severe but he knew how to smile.
Left: Rocky models his 'tubes' - you can also see
part of his scar from tumour removal.

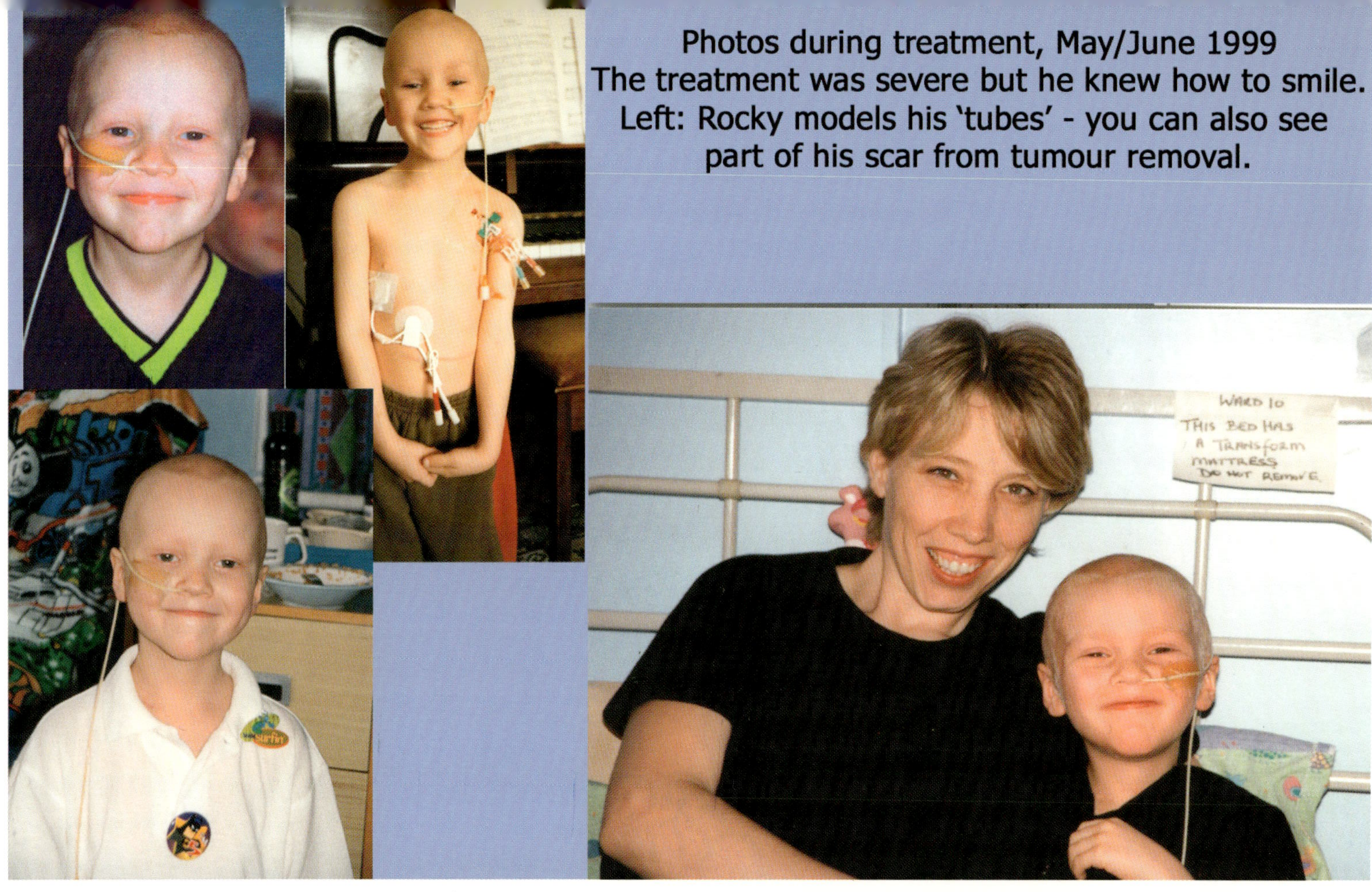

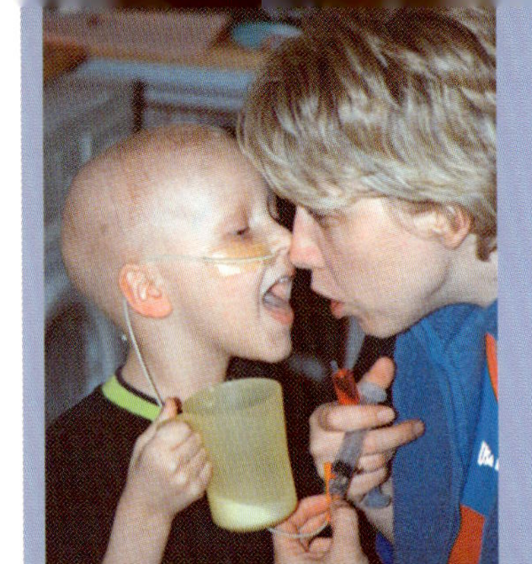

Top Left: When being given medicines down his nasal tube, Rocky preffered to drink a glass of milk.
Bottom Left : The daily visits from his sisters made a huge difference to Rocky.
Bottom Right: Rocky about to have radiotherapy July 1999. Most of the marks on his back are ink, but the smaller ones are permanent tattoos.

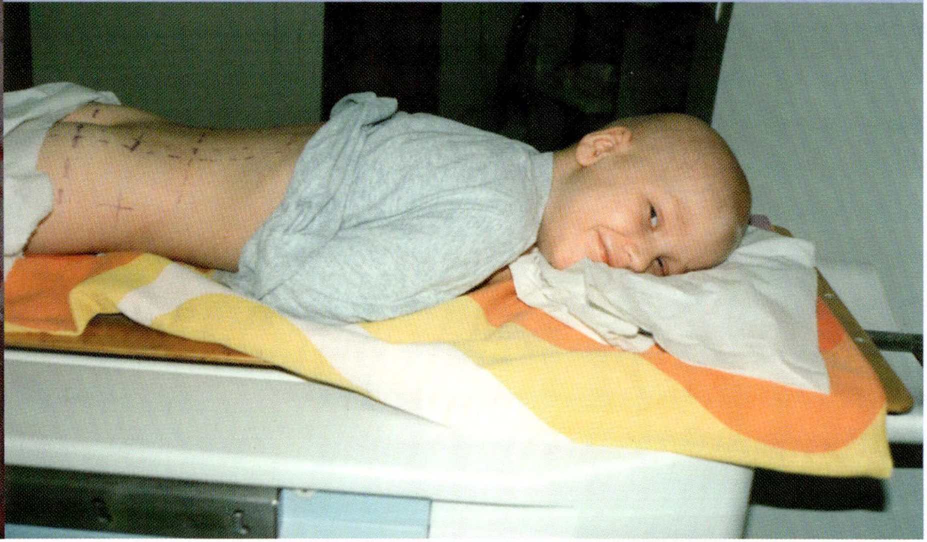

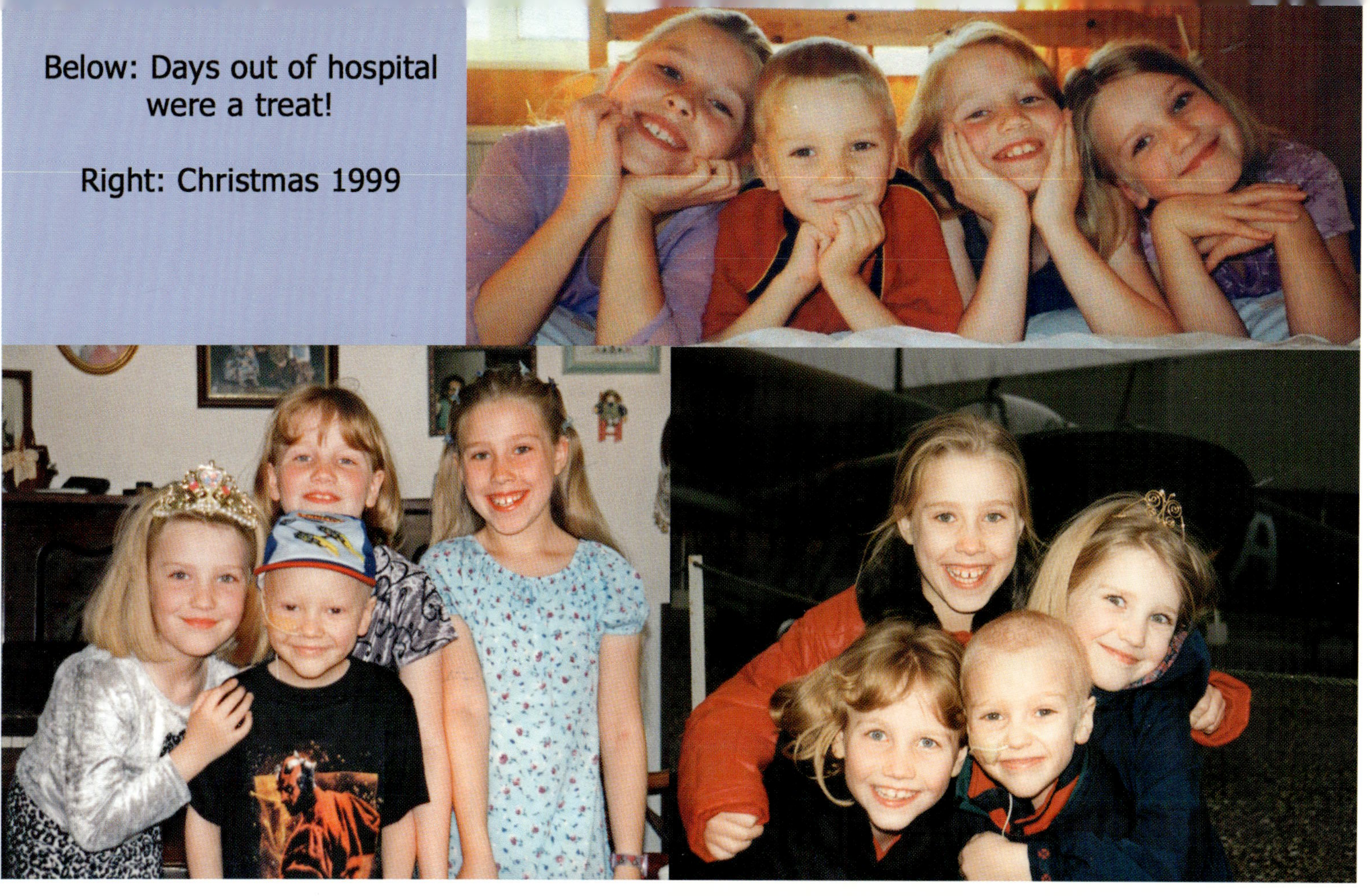

Below: Days out of hospital were a treat!

Right: Christmas 1999

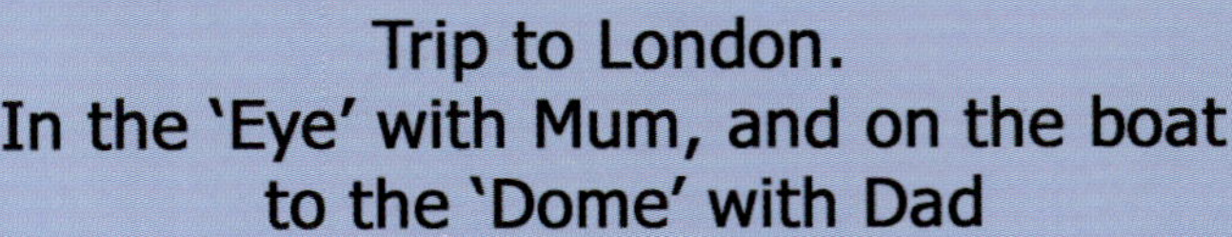

Trip to London.
In the 'Eye' with Mum, and on the boat
to the 'Dome' with Dad

Top Left & Mid: Euro-Disney. Sept 1999. *Top Right:* Rocky holding 'Speckle' (Melody's rabbit) *Bottom Left:* Dessert at a Candelighters Lodge in Bridlington. *Bottom Right:* Rocky presents a cheque to Candlelighters.
Next Page : The keepsake card that we gave out at 'Rocky's Big Send Off'.

"A hero's strength is measured by his heart"

Rocky Josiah Redman went the distance from 8th May 1994 to 27th June 2001 and found a hero's welcome waiting for him at the end of his journey.

19 *We'll always have Paris*

Everyone has a wish.

Whatever you think your wishes are, when your child gets cancer you quickly change your focus.

For Pauline and I, we just wanted our son to get better but I am not sure that Rocky ever focussed on the illness very much. Pauline is a great mother and her input into Rocky helped him maintain a hopeful and cheerful heart.

So, when Rocky was asked what he would wish for I didn't quite know what to expect.

Make a Wish are a fairly well known charity that make wishes come true for very sick children. Pauline's sister contacted them and nominated Rocky for a wish. Shortly afterwards they contacted me and asked to come and see us as a family. The representatives were young, bright and very positive. They explained the work of the charity and asked if they could interview Rocky without us so that they could genuinely ascertain his wishes (rather than ours!)

I wondered what he would ask for. I wanted to go to the USA – but I didn't know if he did! You read of sick children being rushed off to Florida for the holiday of a lifetime and I guess I just thought this was maybe our turn.

When they asked Rocky for three wishes he gave the following:

1. "I want to see a Space Shuttle launched". This one won maximum points with me as they all take off in Florida – and I wanted to see one too!

2. "I want to meet Luke Skywalker". This one also left me hopeful because they were making Star Wars movies again, and maybe a trip to California would let us all meet some of the cast?

3. "I want to feed a shark". Now where on earth did that come from? I don't remember him expressing any interest in sharks before, although I think he had a rubber one that he used to play with. In fact I remember that it had a huge cavernous mouth big enough to get all of my suitably sized nose in. That's right, Rocky's shark regularly fed on my nose!

The rep explained that they had to go away now and write a report on Rocky's wishes and that a committee would decide whether they could grant his. This would take about a month but the wish would be fulfilled very quickly after that if they decided to go ahead.

We were grateful that they were willing to consider Rocky and they went away leaving us to get on with treatment.

The months passed and nothing happened. We didn't hear anything and so we just assumed that nothing was going to come of it. Eventually we got a call apologising for the delay. We were told that they had been unable to get insurance for Rocky to travel to the USA and so weren't able to help. Our family jaunt to America was not going to happen, but then something else wonderful did.

In most hospital units the ward clerk just handles the phone and the paperwork. Not so on Ward 10. This lovely lady also coordinated 'wishes' for another charity. This one was called "Make a Dream (MAD)" and was based locally. As we approached the end of chemotherapy we were asked whether Rocky would like a trip to EuroDisney, Paris or Legoland, Denmark. They were a smaller charity and offered simpler short haul trips so that they could help as many children as possible. Rocky chose Euro-Disney and in a few weeks we were off on a 3 day trip to Paris. It all had to be booked as late as possible in the hope that Rocky would be well enough to go. As you can imagine, MAD were used to cancellations.

The charity arranged everything. We flew from Leeds/Bradford airport to Charles De Gaulle, Paris. They had also arranged for us to go into the cockpit and talk to the pilot. Rocky loved that – and so did I.

At this time Rocky was using a wheel chair – he could walk short distances but became tired very quickly and was prone to leg pain.

Local authority rules meant that Rocky's wheelchair that had been provided could not be taken with us, so the charity arranged for one to be brought to the plane, but unfortunately the locals had some form of mix up and it never happened. I had to carry him across the airport, so the girls had to help Pauline with the luggage. The airport is the size of a small town!

A mini-bus was waiting for us to take us to the hotel and a very friendly driver helped us on our way to the hotel. The hotel had allegedly reserved a wheelchair for us, but one wasn't available when we arrived. It would only have been for use in the hotel and so wouldn't have helped us get to Disney.

The Hotel's pool was shut but an alternative nearby hotel was 'pool sharing' so after arriving we ate a meal and then went via shuttle bus to another hotel to use the pool.

This involved a lot of carrying of Rocky.

The next day we had our first venture into EuroDisney.

The shuttle bus dropped us off nearby and we had to walk about ¼ mile into the complex. Once there, we knew we would be able to hire a wheelchair for the day (deposit £50). Unfortunately the wheelchair hire area was not at the entrance but quite a way inside. Yet again, a lot of carrying Rocky was involved.

Once we had wheels the whole experience changed. Rocky had a priority pass that got us all straight onto whatever ride he wanted. We all went on most rides, but if they looked particularly sickly I stood and watched! Pauline has always loved rollercoasters and I have always hated them. Rocky took after his mum!

I particularly remember entering a Star Wars shuttle ride. It was a virtual experience (the shuttle was on a hydraulic base). Inside we saw the huge view screen in front of us that looked like an enormous window. We lifted off from inside the Death Star and shot into the endless realms of outer space. The shuttle dived, banked and rolled. My internal gyroscope lost all connection with the real world and my stomach began to drift weightlessly as if it were some cosmic flotsam or jetsam consigned to the wastes of space.

I couldn't get off quick enough.

Rocky stayed on for his 5th ride. His special pass allowed that and the staff encouraged him. Unfortunately, one family did nothing but complain all the way through his second ride that he was allowed to stay on. It ruined his second ride and I am sure it ruined theirs too. The difference was that they only had the one ride that they had ruined but Rocky had a few more!

I am sure it was the cocktails of anti-sickness drugs that Rocky had lived on for the previous months that had conditioned his system to not be affected. Even the girls came off after a couple of rides!

Rocky thought this ride was amazing – he wanted to take it home. His interest in Star Wars was obviously part of it, but he loved the sensation too.

After the shuttle I was careful about which rides I tried.

I remember that we all enjoyed "Honey, I shrunk the audience" where our feet had compressed air blown over them and the whole auditorium convinced us we had changed size. I also enjoyed "It's a small world" with Rocky. This ride was very gentle, but had lots of different characters from Disney movies and the wider world. I cried so much on that ride – not because it was scary but because it was emotionally moving! Pauline made fun of me and thought it was "a bit cheesy". There again, I have always done cheese.

Disney staff couldn't have been better, but their star employee was of course best of all. We all went up to meet Mickey Mouse. He made a big fuss of Rocky, but an even bigger fuss of Pauline. The unreality of meeting a cartoon character from your childhood when you are an adult is bizarre to the extreme. When this imaginary character then seems to show genuine compassion for you and your son, reality blurs into fiction. This time it was Pauline's turn to cry; the big-eared legendary rodent hugged her and for a moment it seemed like he wouldn't let go. Pauline thought it a very embarrassing concept to cry when hugged by Mickey Mouse, but it did happen.

The wheelchair and the VIP pass say a lot about you, of course, and everyone was very helpful.

Disney is of course all about imagination.

Cancer is very real.

Thank God, He is real too.

After great comfort in the hotel and wonderful buffet breakfasts that filled us up until tea time, we had another 2 days in the park. We saw the parades, and the fireworks. We walked in the footsteps of Indiana Jones, Pirates and Peter Pan. We had more fun than I can describe. Our girls had the time of their lives and for Rocky it was the stuff dreams were made of.

For Pauline and me it was a rollercoaster ride – not the sort that spins and throws your body but the type that plays havoc with your emotions. I also ached with having to carry Rocky for such great distances each day.

As our chauffeur came to take us back to the airport there was much to try and process in our minds. We took off and did a loop over Paris. We were low enough to see the Arc de Triomphe illuminated in all its evening glory. This is without doubt the most wonderful thing I have ever seen out of an aeroplane window.

Arielle would have been just 7 years old and she got some sort of pressure issue in her ears. In all of her life, I don't ever remember her crying in pain like she did on that flight. It took about fifteen or twenty minutes before it stopped. She was tearful but got over into quickly. Very quickly we were back in Leeds, where we climbed in our Space Wagon and drove back home to York. We were tired and emotionally zapped, but we had accumulated another set of great memories that my aching arms could not overpower.

The charity had done us proud, and over the years we have never forgotten the wonderful times we had in those three days.

Emotions are stretched, squashed, pulled, pushed, locked up and released at times of pressure in life. This pressure time made us go through every feeling in the book, but we always chose to respond positively to each day. This attitude and the sense that God was with us made every day possible – just!

Wishes and dreams can come true.

20 *Trials & Tribulations*

On September 27th, ten months after our journey had started, I returned to work.

By this time a new regime had come in at my employer's head office and I was welcomed back at full basic pay and at my old rank. However the company had filled my job – they obviously couldn't leave it empty, and as a percentage of my pay came from shop performance and someone else was getting that portion, I wasn't earning all that I could. I was an "operations manager without port-folio". My line manager was wonderful; he tried to break me in slowly and asked me what responsibilities I would like to take on.

To say that I got up to speed quickly is an understatement; I knew that I was adding something to the business. The real difficulties were not associated with taking on the work again, but with leaving my family. Having been together so close through such an intense period in our lives the tear of being apart was the biggest strain.

One of the hardest things I had to do in my first month back at work was ask for a day off to conduct Harry's funeral. Our friend's fabulous little boy had died at the end of October. I was given the great honour of presiding at the celebration of his life. Having our own little boy recovering from treatment from this terrible disease made the funeral very meaningful for us. Someone suggested to me that I was the last person on earth to officiate because of my proximity to the disease, but the reality was the opposite. Our boy was returning to health, but we had nearly been boxed in down the same cul-de-sac as our friends and we did at least understand their journey – even if we hadn't arrived at the same destination.

One of the events at the clinic was to submit a urine test once a month to check for markers that would indicate active cancer cells. This test was to look for a relapse. For a boy with whom we had already been told that there was only palliative treatment for a relapse, this test's only purpose was to give a death sentence. The urine had to be handed in and it took a week to know whether it was positive or negative.

We decided not to take this test.

The senior consultant wanted to talk to us about this. Ian, or Professor Ian as we must now address him, is a great man, but he was very concerned with our decision. Pauline and I had to explain our thought process to him and in the end he had to agree that the test told us nothing good. We assured him that if we thought something was wrong, we would agree to a test, but that the psychological pressure of waiting every month to know the result was too much to put us through. I remember Pauline saying that if something was wrong, we would know!

Although off treatment, immune suppression lasts a long time afterwards, and at the time Harry died Rocky was fighting an infection in his Hickman line. The physical hole in the chest that allows the pipe in is itself a doorway to infection and sometimes the pipe becomes a conduit. Fortunately a course of antibiotics cleared it up in a few days. Although things were looking up physically, Rocky continued to be ill a lot, just with little things like this. In fact, the line infection returned after only two weeks and we had to start antibiotics all over again.

The big plus of these infections was that when Pauline turned around to the consultant and said "can't we just have the line taken out?" she agreed. Whereas it was protocol to leave the Hickman line in for 12 months after the end of treatment, it was essential to overcome these infections and one sure fire way was to remove the line. The 12 month rule came from the reality that most children relapse within that period, and it saves the trauma of having to fit one again.

By the time Rocky was scheduled to have the line out, he was on his third line infection – despite regular daily cleaning of the wound and piping. With this last infection, his symptoms were so reminiscent of when cancer first appeared. What was worse was that I was dressing him one day and discovered a small lump near to the scar from his operation. Pauline's nursing experience kicked in and said the word 'hernia'. It was next to a scar and apparently not too unusual. I had been ready to panic (thinking of Harry) but Pauline's expertise made me realise that her argument made sense. A quick run over to the clinic confirmed her diagnosis!

It amazed me that Rocky had his line out 365 days after he had it put in. It was an early Christmas present, and we were in a very different position to that of the previous year.

Rocky woke up in the same bay, in the same recovery room, outside the same theatre with the same nurse that he did previously. This time, instead of being limp and almost lifeless, he grinned from ear to ear, said "Yes! Yes! Yes!", asked to be shown his line (we brought it home in a bag) and started singing "Free, Free, Free at last, I thank God almighty I'm free at last". It was one of those magic moments when we should have had the camcorder.

When I wrote to my email list telling them of the removal of Rocky's line I said "Thank God that we are not looking at the grave this year". That summed up our gratitude and our expectation of total deliverance. We were about to celebrate Christmas again – thank God!

You can imagine that we made a lot of Christmas – and we did, but that year December 31st was Millennium Eve and we celebrated extra hard because it was the end of an era. The end of a millennium was also the end of a chapter in our lives. I had the barbeque out from about 8pm and we partied through to the early hours, grateful that we had enjoyed yet another Christmas and amongst all our momentous days celebrated this significant one together.

Just before being off work I had completed 95% of an assessment which would play a part in my next promotion. Whilst being away my folder had 'gone missing'. I had to start again with the process, but my line manager could remember signing off most of it and so he let me advance through in a professional manner and at an appropriate rate. I took on a couple of projects and achieved the required standards, thereby completing my assessment and was able to send the folder to head office.

I confirmed that head office had received my folder, but a few weeks later when updating my training records they had lost it. I began to think that someone didn't want me to advance in the company.

I had joined the company at Doncaster and been promoted from there to York. Now they wanted me back at Doncaster. I didn't have any choice but to take the longer trip each day, but my time there gave new opportunities including preparing occasional reports for presentation to the directors. Very quickly the rhythms of work became the drumbeat to my life again.

Every week I took my day off to take Rocky to the clinic. The weekly visit kept me close to what was going on and helped ground me in the reality of life without slipping off into the parallel universe of retailing.

During this time though, we were still feeding Rocky every which way we could, but at least now we didn't have any nasty cancer cells or noxious treatment fighting our progress. It was a joy to see him put on weight and a lot of hair on the top of his head. His straight blond hair returned curly! Apparently curly hair can be a common side effect of chemotherapy on children. Pauline and I thought about all those expensive perms she had in the 1980's and realised that a course of chemotherapy might have delivered the same result!

You might think that after losing the Hickman line we would rush off to the swimming baths, but Rocky had a string of chest infections over the next six weeks and such indulgences were not to be.

The surprise that did come along was another trial that was 'post-treatment'. The researchers had come to the view that extraordinarily high doses of Vitamin A or Retinoic Acid might have a long term benefit to the child, and so we opted for the trial. There was a long list of side effects but the only one that Rocky seemed to have was dry skin – a little flakiness and sore patches. The main thing was that it didn't need injections and so he was happy.

The retinoic acid continued for some time and as it built up in Rocky's system the side effects got worse, although they were not debilitating. For a while his eyes became very sore with conjunctivitis, he had more diarrhoea and abdominal pain.

Seven months after the end of treatment Rocky finally topped 20kg in weight. He had put on 33% of body mass since his lowest ebb 14 months before, but he still had another 3kg to go before he reached his weight at diagnosis. When being weighed at the clinic one week in March 2000, Rocky had the unusual experience of being examined by the surgeon who had performed both of his operations. He didn't normally cover the clinic. He made some comment about how good Rocky's scar was from the removal of the tumour, and Pauline pointed out the 'big red blob' where his line had been might fade in time. His words were so encouraging when he said that 'I don't think anyone will notice when he has hair on his chest'.

To the best of my knowledge this was the first time anyone in the medical profession spoke of Rocky growing up. We loved it!

What had happened to the kids' schooling? This is a good question. Without doubt, our girls were way ahead of others their age by cruising through the Accelerated Christian Education curriculum. The plan had been that whilst Pauline was in hospital with Rocky, I would supervise their learning in the mornings. This didn't happen as much as it should have done, so when Rocky's treatment was over Pauline took back the reins and school started again in earnest.

At this time, Pauline started to teach Rocky the basics, but didn't work him too hard because his stamina was not great. What was clear from day one was that his aptitude for Maths was remarkable.

If Pauline and I were talking about money or anything like that and talked through calculations aloud we would often find that Rocky had them worked out before us. Managing Rocky's learning was a little challenging because he couldn't face a full day 'in school' so he had to be allowed doses of Cartoon Network on cable TV. The girls, however, were quickly back up to speed and it would seem that the months of upheaval had little impact on their learning.

Back in my 'shopkeeper' role, a new store was due to open at Harrogate. I joined the team as Operations Manager and supervised the set-up and opening of the new store. A new store was just what I needed and gave me the maximum opportunity express myself in a creative way. This was a much better journey than Doncaster too!

21 *The Wish We Forgot*

Do you remember those wishes Rocky made?

The Make a Wish Foundation did!

There was no way anyone was going to insure Rocky to travel across the Atlantic on a long haul flight, but there is more than one way to skin a cat.

One of the Make A Wish team read in the papers that the "George Lucas Star Wars Exhibition" was coming to London from the USA. They saw "Star Wars" and thought of Rocky!

Out of the blue we got a phone call offering to grant the second two of Rocky's wishes.

The idea was to spend three days in London, stopping at the Tara Kensington (a very nice hotel indeed!) One day was to be spent at the Star Wars exhibition at the Barbican, with a morning at the London Aquarium, where Rocky would be allowed to feed the sharks.

To add a bit more excitement for us, we were to get a trip on the London Eye (which funnily enough is just outside the London Aquarium) and a day at the Millennium Dome.

For those of you who have already forgotten, the Dome was already a huge political embarrassment, a white elephant in the eyes of the media, but is now the successful O2 Arena.

A boat ride from the London Eye to the Dome was included and so we prepared ourselves with open minds to our trip!

The train journey was great family fun. We did, of course, take our NHS wheelchair this time as we were staying in the country. Having said that, I think it fair to say we would have taken it anyway after our trip to Paris!

Getting about with a wheelchair on the London underground was quite a challenge. All of us should take a moment when we are next there to think how we would manage in a wheelchair.

Arriving at the Tara in Kensington released lots of warm, fuzzy memories from the days in which I used to buy and sell Hifi equipment. The annual "Radio Show" in London was held at a range of top hotels and the Tara used to host Panasonic & Technics, so I always used to go there.

The hotel couldn't do enough for us, but the big surprise was from the foundation. We expected them to welcome us because they said they would, but we didn't expect a room full of Star Wars toys. Some toy retailer in London had donated one of everything and we lost count of the number of items Rocky was given. I think there were something between 40 and 50 different toys.

It goes without saying that Rocky wasn't without amusement.

Of all of the action figures and space ships that Rocky had the one thing I remember the most is his "Jar Jar Binks" rucksack. It looked like the character from "The Phantom Menace" and had those floppy ears. It was a bag, but looked more like an alien perched on his back!

The toys were so numerous and occupied so much room that it wasn't possible for us to take them home with us – they had to be couriered to our home after the trip!

Dinner was at Planet Hollywood. They had donated an 'everything on the menu' visit for Rocky, so the six of us ordered anything we wanted and it didn't cost a bean. Rocky and his sisters especially enjoyed the colourful range of non-alcoholic cocktails in the special glasses – and of course Rocky got to keep his glass to bring home. The staff were brilliant with one of them giving Rocky a juggling demonstration.

The following morning we went to the Barbican.

A huge Naboo fighter filled a section of the exhibit. There were space ships, models and costumes of every description. Perhaps the most interesting part of the exhibit was the Darth Vader costume in a glass case. A motion sensor turned on a recording of DV's famous 'breathing' when anyone approached the cabinet.

Rocky had his photo taken with R2D2 and with every piece of memorabilia that you can imagine. There were masks to try on and costumed staff interacting with visitors. In fact Luke Skywalker was probably the only one not there, but Rocky was enjoying himself so much he never noticed.

Every item on show was identified by Rocky. Occasionally I would make a comments about which movie or planet an article was from only to be corrected by my son who was, of course, right about it all. He had become a Star Wars expert, and being in such an amazing exhibit was like a dream come true for him. As much as the exhibition was open to the public, as far as Rocky was concerned this was an answer to prayer for him alone.

A display of alien masks that visitors could try on was a hoot for Rocky. Not only did the adult size masks look hilarious on his little body, but he knew the origin of every one and could usually quote dialogue from each character – however insignificant to the plot.

We went out to eat on the roof top café area and Rocky felt well enough to chase the pigeons!

It was a great day! When we eventually had to leave the Barbican, Rocky wasn't annoyed or begging to stay – he had enjoyed every moment and was fulfilled. He also knew a lot about his own stamina and when he needed to rest he didn't fight it hard. He saved his energy to fight the disease, not the requirement to leave a building.

We had a waiter in the hotel that the children became very attached to and even that helped make the break a memorable one. Our suite of adjoining rooms was excellent. Pauline and I had much needed space, but the kids were never more than an adjoining door apart from us.

The second day we went to the Aquarium. You would have thought that the staff there had nothing to do but look after us. If you have never been to this aquarium it is without doubt a most excellent place to visit. The rare breeds of fish are incredible. Rocky watched as divers got in tanks with fish, we all stroked rays and got close to all the research projects that happen in the private areas of the aquarium.

Most stunning was when they took Rocky to the sharks. Without being prompted he stuck his hands in the bucket of fish and began feeding the sharks. The staff spent quality time making sure he did things that he would never forget, but most interestingly to us, absolutely nothing fazed him. A shark leaping up out of the water made me jump but Rocky was just fascinated and enjoyed every minute. He was like a sponge, absorbing everything around him and storing it inside himself for future use.

When we were about to leave the Aquarium staff there had friends at the London Eye so they went out and got our tickets. Queuing time was about 30 minutes once tickets were bought, so they really helped us by sorting them out in advance. After my space shuttle journey in France I wasn't sure whether I wanted to go on the big wheel. But the decision was taken away from me because they wouldn't allow his wheelchair onboard. They also wouldn't store his wheelchair, so one of us had to stay below and watch. The decision made, I sat and tried to catch them in the lens of my camera whilst my four children enjoyed the view with Mum.

Having had that singular view of London, the family joined me in the queue for the boat ride to the dome. Again this was just next to the eye, so we had very little distance to walk.

The weather was glorious, so the boat ride was memorable. Rocky and his sisters enjoyed every minute and we travelled the most convenient way possible to the Dome. Our children have always appreciated life and each new experience. It cannot be overstated however just how much fun a riverboat ride can be on a sunny day in London.

Built on the Greenwich Meridian to celebrate the new millennium, the Dome was split into 14 zones that were themed into groups around the titles "Who we are", "What we do" and "Where we live". Once we arrived at the Dome we had our tickets prepaid and we entered to see a trapeze display in the centre of the building. The Body Zone was captivating for Rocky – he loved the way he could run through a mock up of the heart and found loads of exhibits where he could press buttons and get a response – a little boy's dream!

The only mistake we made was making this just an afternoon trip – there was so much to do in the Dome it needed at least a full day. It did at least mean that we were not bored in our visit, but we had to miss out whole chunks that may have merited further examination. Despite all the efforts put into the Dome for children, with a strong emphasis on education, I think Pauline and I probably enjoyed it even more than they did. We came away with a view that the only thing wrong with the Dome was the media attitude to it; the media succeeded in their campaign to undermine the Dome in the minds of those whose taxes had paid for it.

When we returned to the hotel each evening, we were truly tired. We squeezed so much into those 'wish days' that all of us slept well.

The level of 'adventure' that Rocky experienced on that trip was absolutely fabulous. From the train journey (which Pauline made into an exciting expedition) to breakfast in a high quality hotel – these were all mind blowing experiences for a little boy. Little things always made Rocky happy, so big things like this trip were amazing to him.

We didn't get our trip to see the shuttle launch and couldn't make America, but we did have a wonderful time and the creativity and imagination of the "Make a Wish" foundation made a little boy from York very happy indeed.

I have always enjoyed the return train journey far more than the outward one. This was no different, but we had so many new and wonderful memories to talk about that there was no pause in the adventure until we arrived home in York. Coming home may not in itself be an adventure, but with all the weeks in hospital we had all learned to appreciate it so much that we let out a cheer as we entered the door!

As Rocky fell asleep, I couldn't help but consider how much of the events of the last three days had been a specific answer to his own prayers. Sometimes I heard him pray – and many of those prayers were for other people, but some of them were for himself. I wondered if he had asked God about Star Wars and sharks? I like to think that God heard him and prepared the answer, unbeknown to Mum and Dad.

It would be perverse beyond belief to ever say there were perks out of having cancer – but there were some special opportunities and wonderful memories. "Make A Wish" certainly made sure that we had a great deposit in our memory banks from these three days.

When treatment seems unending and the constant pressure unabated, it is good to fix in your minds that blessing is just around the corner. We had many blessings at this point in our lives and it is a good discipline to remember them. The Psalmist (Ps103) reminds us not to forget any of the benefits we have received. This episode was another set of benefits and as I am recounting them to you I am also being grateful for them to God.

22 *Rocky Goes Flying*

One of Rocky's uncles was in the Territorial Army. He was a quiet type, but a kind man. I guess that we didn't know him well, but like everyone who knew us, he was moved by Rocky's journey. Unlike many, he wasn't just moved; he tried to do something to give our son a treat.

He sent a message that he was trying to arrange a day out for Rocky with the Army. As much as we accepted this I am not sure that we expected it would ever happen. Lots of people said things but many didn't mean them. So when the appointed day came around, the grandeur and excitement of the day was almost more than we could take in. Uncle John had really pulled off an impressive day out.

It was April 14th 2000.

We arrived at Dishforth in the morning to an official welcome. This Army Air Corps base had previously been an RAF station. Rocky got a tour of the base in an armoured personnel carrier. An instructor took us to the obstacle course and the children were let loose to enjoy themselves. They all thought it was great and had a fabulous time, although Rocky's involvement was limited by his physical stamina.

We were given a meal in the officer's mess and Rocky was presented with a boy's size flying jacket. It had a pilots wings and really looked the part. The flying jacket was going to be necessary because the next thing was Rocky was going to do was go up in an army Gazelle helicopter.

I have to say at this point that I had an experience of helicopters that I hadn't enjoyed. Some years before, I had flown into the British Grand Prix at Silverstone in a private Sea King helicopter with about 20 seats. I found the experience the reverse to flying in a jet. Normally the dodgy parts are take offs and landings, but in a helicopter they are fine – it is the travelling forwards that's the problem. The only thing worse is when they just hover!

So when Rocky was only allowed to take one parent with him, this was a relief. I graciously, and without consideration of the obvious deprivation I was about to experience, allowed my wife the honour of the flight.

The media were there photographing Rocky in his flight suit and helmet with his mum. The Yorkshire Post were taking photos as well as the Army publicity department. They asked me questions about Rocky's disease and his current health. I overheard the officer in charge briefing the reporters. Whereas I cannot remember his exact words the sense of it was that every boy's dream was to be in the Army and as soon as the Army had heard that our little boy was *dying* and would *never be able to fulfil his dream* they stepped in.

The Army were very kind that day, and Rocky's Uncle John had been brilliant – not many men could have pulled of such a treat for their nephew! However, my realisation was that in fact we were there for the Army's sake and not for our son's. This was a huge PR campaign and Rocky was a handy cancer sufferer. I suppose human nature looks for these opportunities, but the reality of their motivation still came as a disappointment.

My boy wasn't dying and I didn't like these men saying it. I found it most infuriating that a man felt he could just brief someone that my son was dying! My son was living, and we would continue to fight for life.

Although I took time to spell 'neuroblastoma' to the reporter, the story in the newspaper the next day said 'leukaemia'. It appeared that army briefings had more weight than those of a parent.

The helicopter lifted off the ground and hovered no more than two metres above the runway. Several minutes passed during which I wondered if they had a '2 metre high' rule for children under 6. They were of course waiting for permission from the tower to set off. Very quickly Rocky and Pauline were in the sky circling the airfield before heading off to the east coast. At breakneck speed my boy and his mum saw the seaside and back again. I think the flight lasted around half an hour.

Pauline found the flight quite nauseating and only barely kept her stomach contents where it belonged. She was sure that Rocky felt it too and wondered at times if he might fill the cockpit with vomit. However, no space shuttle ride at Disney or real army helicopter could unleash Rocky's stomach contents on the world. Maybe the months of anti-emetic drugs in his system gave him the resistance he needed to make it through that fabulous ride.

All the time he was being treated for cancer we had kept that toy 'helicopter gunship' nearby to remind us of God's hovering power. Those hovering Gazelles helped keep our troops safe in battle, and Rocky had survived treatment and was recovering because of prayer to a hovering God. After all that Rocky had endured, he actually got to ride in the physical manifestation of a spiritual truth.

This was a day to remember and we weren't going to let the fact that our little boy was being used for a PR campaign stop us enjoying it. We bought a few copies of the newspaper and the media people sent us a wonderful print of the photo used in the newspapers – it is truly one of the best we ever had.

Pauline and Rocky made a bit of a splash in the local media again!

23 Let the Good Times Roll

I was in the back of a large American car. It had to be American because we just don't have them that big in England.

I looked out of the window and we drove over a railway line. The earth was slightly red and a big factory was in the background. The rail track was open, the crossing had no barriers or gates. There was a goods train coming along the line. This was definitely the USA.

I found myself facing a group of men. I sensed they were elders, leaders in the church. They looked at me expecting me to say something. I felt under scrutiny.

Not being able to stand the tension of the silence I opened my mouth and said "so this is Mississippi?"

They looked at me as if I was mad.

"This is Missouri", one of them said, "but we are near the Mississippi".

I awoke. It had been another one of those dreams that I get occasionally. It was more than a natural dream – I had to go there, but where had I been in my dream?

I ran downstairs and turned on the computer. I trawled the internet for the words Mississippi and Missouri. I discovered that the river Mississippi was on the border of the state of Missouri – so there was a whole side of the state that was in fact near the Mississippi.

A couple of weeks later a friend dropped round after church. She never used to watch TV very much so I was quite taken aback when she asked me to turn the TV on. She wanted to see a programme about genetically modified foods, so I turned the TV on for her and sat down to watch.

On the screen was a factory set amongst a reddish earth. In front of the factory was an open railway line. A goods train was coming along it.

It was the scene from my dream.

I began to point at the screen and tried to stutter out some words, but my friend thought I was having some sort of epileptic convulsion.

I finally forced out the words "It's my dream", as the caption appeared on the screen: "St Louis Missouri – Home of Monsanto Chemicals".

I shared this with my wife and my Pastor. Both agreed that I really did need to go to St Louis. The only thing I knew about that city was the old song from the Judy Garland movie of the same name "Meet me in St Louis". Maybe God would meet me there?

I wondered if this was a continuation of my last trip when I had heard about building an Ark? When I gave Google the words "Build an Ark AND St Louis" it came back with an invitation to see how they built the St Louis Arch. Apparently the largest building in the state is the St Louis Arch – a 630 foot tall, 630 foot wide stainless steel sculpture with an internal elevator that allows you to visit the top.

Completed in 1965 the Arch commemorates Thomas Jefferson and the westward expansion of the United States. Without making the trip I wasn't going to find out any more. I had some holidays accrued so with Pauline's blessing I bought a transatlantic ticket and set off chasing a dream.

On September 12th 2000 I flew to St Louis. The weather was wonderful as I sat there for a week praying under a huge stainless steel arch.

I think the total break did me good, but the important thing was that I was practising responding to God's prompting.

I knew no one there and had no contact with anyone, so I read my Bible and prayed and kept going around the Arch exhibits.

I thought God was speaking to me to go and visit the church named after the Arch. At the time there were over 600 churches in the St Louis yellow pages. I looked through them all. None of them were called Arch Church or anything similar. However on my visit to the exhibit "How we built the Arch" I discovered that whereas everyone called it the 'St Louis Arch' or the 'Jefferson National Expansion Memorial', it was also known as the 'Gateway Arch'.

You guessed well. There was one church in the directory called Gateway. Funnily enough we had one in York too – had I travelled thousands of miles to visit a church of the same name as one only a mile from my house!

I went to Gateway Church that Sunday. It was a well attended modern building on the outskirts of the city. The newly arrived in America taxi driver took me a long way away and then tried to demand extra money to get me where I had asked in the first place.

When I got there, the service was enjoyable and even involved a break for coffee and doughnuts. The preacher stood up to speak. He said that he was going to continue on with his series of dealing with difficult questions.

'This week's question is', he said, 'what exactly do you say to a man who has just been told that his son has cancer?'

You can imagine the shock I felt. You have a dream about a strange place. You go there and find a church full of strangers. You are only there once and yet the preacher asks a question that is referring to you – in fact statistically you will be the only person in the room who can answer it!

I stood to my feet and raised my arm. 'Excuse me', I shouted.

It was at this moment that I felt stupid, ridiculous and another twenty adjectives that typify that feeling you get when you stick out like a sore thumb.

He asked me who I was and what I wanted.

I still am very good at projecting my voice.

"I have travelled from England to answer your question – because I am that man", I shouted.

I was allowed up to the platform to speak and told simply of our experience with Rocky and that fortunately I had known what I needed to know – that God is good, that He didn't 'have it in for me' and that He would be with us.

I was thanked for my contribution and sat down.

I found the preacher remarkable, because no one likes to be interrupted from the floor, especially by someone who is not part of the local body, but he was very gracious.

He carried on talking about the question and referred to an incident that had happened in the church a couple of years previously. It seemed that a teenager called Billy-Bob had developed cancer and died. At his funeral the whole family had come together and as a result most of his relatives had believed in Jesus for their personal salvation. The preacher went on to say that we see that this horrible situation was actually the will of God because by the loss of Billy-Bob something like 16 people had found God.

Oops.

I stood up again. That hand was in the air. Before I could stop myself I had said "Excuse me!"

I began to preach. I told them how that cancer was not a result of the will of God but of the fall of man. I said that all evil in the world had come about because of our rebellion and that God did not make us sick to bring about something better. In fact the Bible tells us in Romans 8:28 that in all things God is working for the good of those who love Him. It was in the evil of cancer and the horror of bereavement that God turned things around for good by drawing people close to Him. It worked out well, but not because the cancer was from God – it worked out well despite the cancer! I then really dropped myself in it by saying that it was tantamount to blasphemy to blame a child's cancer on God.

Now preachers don't like being interrupted, but they certainly don't like being corrected!

I knew that I was in imminent danger of being manhandled by the large American hands of the ushers. Any minute now the elders were going to throw me out of the building.

It went silent.

After a pause the preacher thanked me again and continued.

He told the congregation that God had been gracious enough to send a man all the way from England who actually had experience of this question. He also said that he was grateful that I had corrected him and that he never wanted to hear anyone else in that church ever say that Billy-Bob's cancer had come from God.

The relief I felt was tangible. I kept my big mouth shut for the rest of the service.

At the end the Pastor came up to me and thanked me for visiting. He told me that he wanted to take me out for lunch but that it was his elderly mother's birthday and he had promised her a family occasion. He asked if I would be willing to have one of the elders of the church entertain me for lunch. I gratefully accepted.

As the social mingling at the end of the service started to wind down, an elder approached me. He told me that they always took visiting preachers to a particular restaurant in St Louis for lunch but he had just heard that week about a new eatery that had opened outside of the city limits and would I mind if he took me there as he wanted to try it out? I gratefully accepted.

I sat in the back of this large American vehicle looking out of the windows as he drove me past the red earth in front of the Monsanto Chemicals factory. There was a goods train in the distance but we crossed the unguarded railway line well in front of it.

I was so amazed by the events of that morning I don't remember what we had for lunch.

I got back to the hotel and emailed Pauline with my report of the day. There was a photo of Rocky waiting for me in my inbox holding a couple of Cherry Bakewells. I laughed at the photo of my curly haired son. Pauline's little boy was holding her favourite cakes in his hands and it was a reminder to me that we had been to the very brink – and made it back.

That was my great adventure of millennium year, but we had many other good times together. Perhaps the most special was a holiday in November at Centre Parcs in the forest when Rocky felt so well that he threw himself into everything with the energy of a child who had never been sick. One afternoon he went on the remote control cars and lost the race. He was so upset that he ran away and we couldn't find him. Eventually I went back to the lodge and there he was! So much energy for a boy who had been so ill!

In fact that week was when Pauline and I actually realised he was well. He wasn't sickly anymore. It was as if we had our boy back

Rocky said to me one Sunday -"What are we going to do at Church today, Dad?"

I replied "We are going to thank God that we are winning your battle". Rocky replied "Oh! We've won that one, Dad!" I stood rebuked.

Arielle went out of her way to play with Rocky and one day Pauline said to Rocky "Isn't Arielle great? She always wants to play with you". Rocky replied "Yes, Mum. When we were in hospital, in the middle of the night when you were asleep, I used to pray in my mind, "God will you make me better please so that Arielle will still have someone to play with?"

I was a bit choked when I heard that. My six year old son had his own faith and his own prayer life.

Our lives had moved on too. There were still the trips to the clinic, but our boy was getting a lot better, the pressure was lifting off.

24 *The R Word*

It was December 2000.

That great annual event was on – the Candlelighters Party. Held that year at the Leeds Armouries, a hundred or more cancer kids and their siblings were being given a great party courtesy of the Candlelighters charity. Rocky was having a whale of a time.

Diarrhoea can only be described as a very messy business. Rocky had a lot during chemo, but had not since. Suddenly, during the party, Rocky had an attack. I took him to the toilet and cleaned him up, but there was something unsettling about it. We couldn't get home quick enough from that party. I was unsettled, but Pauline was *very* unsettled. "This isn't normal", she said to me and in my heart I was rattled.

We had recently moved from weekly clinic to monthly and had long since stopped the regime of testing to look for the dreaded 'R' word – relapse!

Rocky was fine the day after the party but I was ill with influenza for a week or so; then Rocky had some fever symptoms. I hoped that this was Rocky catching my 'flu', but since I was too ill to drive, Pauline took him for an extra clinic visit and offered to have the urine test.

When Rocky was first diagnosed they gave us three weeks. We had Christmas on December 6th 1998 knowing it might be our last but hoping that we would have many more. We celebrated Christmas twice more that year, on the 24th as well as the 25th of December.

After recovering from treatment we enjoyed a further two Christmases in 1999 and 2000, but surprisingly only on the usual dates. So having got Christmas 'out of the way' and entering 2001, Pauline began her usual routine of pantomime, in an effort to carry on as normal despite our deep concerns about Rocky's health.

For a few years Pauline had written, directed and put on local pantos in York and usually played a part too. The usual pattern was not to actually perform it until the very end of the panto season (end of January) over a weekend, usually giving 4 performances. Something like 1500 people would see the panto and we had usually fleeced people for donations to Candlelighters on the way out.

It is impossible as a parent of a child that has fought cancer to not be aware of health implications after treatment. The diminished immunity of the child means that the propensity to pick up anything going around is real. The similarity of symptoms between basic infections and a relapse of cancer is such a reality that every sniffle leaves a question mark.

On the 19th of January we awoke to Rocky coming into our bedroom with a noticeable limp.

At this moment I want to write something like "pause for effect" – the truth is I don't know what to write. I cannot describe how long that moment was when Pauline and I both saw the limp.

It is difficult to describe how an unpleasant eternity can pass between two people's eyes in a second of real time.

Moments like those make me realise that the frightening biblical description of hell as 'eternal death' are very much possible, because even in the temporal limits of this existence a moment can seem forever.

Pauline quizzed him about how he felt and I just remember saying "I'll go and ring the clinic so they know we are coming". It hurt Rocky to be cuddled.

At the Christmas party we had been rattled.

Waking on January 19th we had moved beyond being rattled. We knew.

We took Rocky back to the clinic. He was suffering some intermittent abdominal pain and some back and hip pain. He was asking for Calpol (liquid paracetamol), which was not like Rocky. No one wants to say the R-word, but we just knew.

We hoped not – but we knew.

We prayed that it wasn't – but we knew.

God help us – we knew!

Rocky's consultant Sue's eyes filled with tears and she said those words we hoped that we would never hear. She was concerned that Rocky may be in relapse and requested some tests. She prescribed a more powerful pain killer, DF118, to help Rocky with the pain.

A few days later Rocky had his tests including an ultrasound around his operation area.

Back at home the phone rang – it was the Macmillan nurse. In an emotionless voice, she said that as Rocky was going to die she wanted to come round to arrange his terminal care. Her voice was uncaring, her words were chosen badly, her manner was offensive and unpleasant. We told her not to bother and I immediately rang the consultant back and told her what had happened. Whilst being very apologetic she assured me that the nurse would not contact us again.

Sadly this nurse had dealt with death so much that she had become desensitised to the feelings of those who were trying to cope with it for the first time. She was a professional and had probably helped many people over the years but on that day she had slipped into an automatic mode that made her no use at all. This is a mistake we can all make if we allow our reactions to the circumstances of life to harden our hearts.

The panto was due to start on Friday January 26th. That same morning we set off quickly to Leeds for clinic at the Day hospital. Sue saw us again.

She looked at him very carefully but her examination did not take long. Sue asked a play nurse to take Rocky out so that she could have a talk with us.

Ironically, the urine test that we had avoided for many months was 'unclear'.

The ultrasound was negative; other tests were suggested. Pauline and I both felt it was inappropriate to make Rocky undergo anything invasive.

"You know what I am going to say, don't you? It would seem likely that the cancer is back in his bones. We thought we had got rid of it but neuroblastoma is very difficult. There are some experimental chemos we can try but they are only palliative".

She went on to ask what we wanted to do – there was Martin House, the local children's hospice, and they would of course help us in any way that they could. She said to me that whereas relapse was unpredictable, neuroblastoma was usually fast and that I would need as little as three weeks off work. Her inference was that this time off work might even be enough to cover the funeral.

Her words were clear, kind and with great feeling. Sue is a star.

Those minutes were a whirl and I am not sure about all that happened but I do remember telling her that Pauline was due on stage that night in panto.

We had known, but we were still stunned.

We returned home and I had to have a family meeting with the girls. We told them of the doctor's words, but of our hope in God and that we would now have to fight for Rocky's life all over again. They each committed to pray and make every day as good as possible for Rocky – and also for Mummy.

What were we to do about the panto?

Pauline was not only directing, but she was playing the title role of Cinderella!

What were we to do about the panto?

With tears streaming down her face, Pauline said that she would go ahead as it was the only thing to do. I remember saying that it wasn't true that "the show must go on" but she was right – this should not stop her. It didn't either – she gave a brilliant performance, and the night raised a few thousand pounds for Candlelighters.

The hospice rang – they were marvellous. They sent someone round who was simply lovely. She obviously had a lot of experience with people in our position and she invited us to come over for a day with the idea that if Rocky enjoyed himself we all might like to stop over "for a few days".

That night Pauline and I cried together as she asked me "what are we going to do?" As best as I could I told her that we had experienced miracles along the way and now we needed the big one.

Jesus said *"Peace I leave with you; my peace I give you. I do not give to you as the world gives. Do not let your hearts be troubled and do not be afraid"* John 14:27 NIV.

Christians talk a lot about peace – but at a time when the life of your little boy is at threat and naturally speaking hope has gone, what does that peace amount to? Is this some sort of drug that pacifies the mind and enables the Christian to walk around in a dulled but peaceful state of mind? Is this some sort of nirvana that can be attained by a holy and separate life? Is this peace a result of hours of Bible Study and meditation?

I think the peace that Jesus talked about is peace that you have to fight for!

The last time we took Rocky to the clinic to see Sue was on February 9th. DF118 wasn't helping with the pain, we had to start him on morphine. He wasn't sleeping, eating or walking well. Rocky had severe pain in his elbows, legs and head. I had noticed a bony lump on his back; Sue saw this as likely evidence of activity in his skeleton. Hospital records show this as the date that a relapse certificate was issued for Rocky.

It was at this time that we decided not to have any more blood tests and therefore not to transfuse Rocky. We didn't want him to have any unnecessary discomfort. The hospital could do nothing more; as ever we were in God's hands. We were grateful to them for everything they had done but it was now time to change our emphasis to "don't call us, we'll call you".

Returning home I began a second absence from work. Pauline and I stood together with our daughters, determined to fight with our boy whilst we had strength, knowing that our strength comes from the Lord.

I administered his morphine in the morning and evening with a slow release capsule. In-between he had fast acting morphine pills if necessary. Within a matter of two weeks he had a bony protrusion out of his back. The doctor said that the cancer had probably burst the bone open. Rocky must have felt a lot of pain from this, but we were careful to manage it so that he was awake but not hurting.

Clearly the cancer had been hiding in his skeleton and it had returned with a vengeance.

Pauline has always had 'a high pain threshold'. Rocky inherited that from his Mum too! This time though, he really needed morphine.

Morphine unfortunately has the side effect of paralysing the gut and causing constipation.

Rocky made us laugh when one day he sat on the toilet and shouted "Now that's what I call constipation!" It seemed funny then coming from a six year old; it still sounds funny now.

CHAPTER

25 *The Bad Dream*

The traditional song goes

Row, row, row your boat
Gently down the stream
Merrily, merrily, merrily, merrily
Life is but a dream.

Sure enough, we had done our share of rowing over the last few years. Some have said the lyrics to this ditty are a metaphor for life and the consequences of our personal choices. For people who write dissertations about such matters, it would appear that the line 'life is but a dream' has produced many a long essay.

For us life was very much a real experience – we just thought we must be dreaming sometimes! Our dreamscapes had offered delights and nightmares in various measures, but reality was always with us.

We were a family of six in which Daddy had three girls and Mummy had one little boy.

Don't misunderstand me – we were all very close, but the girls favoured their Dad most of the time, and Rocky always favoured his Mum.

On Thursday March 8th Rocky awoke from a dream. In this dream he complained that his mum repeatedly hit him until he died!

Rocky was not prone to dreams like this and Pauline wasn't prone to violence, but this dream did disturb our little boy, so much so that on that day Rocky changed from sitting cuddled up to his mum and all of a sudden I was the one in favour.

On Saturday 10th Rocky finally made up with Mum and our roles reset themselves.

I must confess that I had really begun to enjoy being the favoured parent, but I felt terrible for Pauline because I could see this was causing her great pain.

That day I was going to church in the evening, but Rocky begged me to stay – so I did. He wouldn't let go of me. At about 8.30pm he just sighed and went limp on me. Polly and I looked across at each other and thought the same thing! For a few seconds we thought he was dead. Then there was a loud noise like a fault in the central heating system and 15 days of bowel movement happened in about 60 seconds!

Pauline said it was a good job I had been there to help. I didn't realise how helpful my panic comments like "Pauline – it's all over the place – what do I do?" were. I made a mental note to remember to be helpfully useless again in the future. I think what she really meant was that my moral support was useful!

It was certainly important that we continued to go to church as much as we could during those days, but it was also important to be sensitive to one another's needs for company and support. I was so glad I had stayed home that night.

After the emptying of his bowels Rocky wanted Mummy back and all was well again!

It was that same week that Rocky moved out of our room. Since his relapse we had him sleep with us. To begin with he slept in our bed (which meant I barely slept at all) and then after a few days he moved to a Z-bed next to ours. This was a reversal of roles! Then after a couple of weeks Rocky decided that he had 'tummy-ache' since he moved into our bedroom but had never had it downstairs – so he moved back.

I was hugely relieved to have our own space again, except that the first night I got up every hour and went to check on him. Soft dad, eh?

From that time we adjusted to Rocky being downstairs in his own bed. His lungs were good and I was sleeping on a hair trigger. One blast of "Father" and I was down there like a shot.

I guess that the lesson I learned through the bad dream experience was that whatever dangers we face, real or imagined, there is a time of healing. Our boy's body was riddled with cancer, but his mind wasn't. He didn't stay angry or upset with his mother – in fact he couldn't stay away from her. Rocky loved me, but he loved Pauline more than words can possibly describe. Those three days were the most hurtful that could be imagined for Pauline at that time, but they passed and all was well again.

We always need to keep rowing merrily down the stream. If we do so with a good attitude it is amazing how not even a bad dream can spoil our journey.

26 Facing the Truth

Sometimes people say that we use faith as a crutch and avoid facing the truth.

The crutch bit is true.

Instead of laying there and dying, disabled and unable to function, by faith we get up and stand again.

I like the crutch thing. When other people are not able to stand, I do because I believe.

Not 'facing the truth' is a lot of baloney though.

Jesus said "*I am the truth*" (John 14:6). When I look at Him I am facing the truth. When I believe the man who is the truth I am facing up to truth.

In a court of law, circumstantial evidence is prone to result in unsafe convictions. My circumstances do not dictate truth. I do not change what I believe because of what I see or experience. Instead I allow what I believe to manage my attitude and response to my circumstances.

After a few drinks some people feel like they can fly – this does not suspend the law of gravity though, and unfortunately some intoxicated people have leapt to their deaths because of the euphoria they experienced.

On June 23rd 2001 I sent the following email to our prayer partners:

The facts:

Rocky is thinner and weaker than he has ever been. If we were to photograph his body in his current state most of you would not be able to look. If you saw him naked advertising for Oxfam famine relief, you would be moved to give generously. Because his skin is all that remains over his bones, he does not have the ability to stand or pull himself up if he slips down in his chair. We have had to source special cushions and a similar mattress to allow him comfort.

He is not eating anything much and hasn't had a bowel movement for 2 weeks. He is very pale and had an incident the other night when his heart rate reached a sustained 160 for at least 15 minutes and he had some sort of "turn".

Since he was prayed for on Saturday, he has slept a lot, and not been out the house. We have therefore reduced his morphine from 2x700mg per day to 2x400mg per day, which he is tolerating without pain.

The truth:

I look at Rocky Josiah and I hear God say "Can these bones live?" I reply "Yes, Lord".

He has survived months longer than the medical profession said. They are bemused at his survival and non-plussed at his ability to reduce morphine consumption from time to time. (This is not possible). Even now his demand is falling. He is still bright, alert when awake, and able to smile, laugh and make amusing observations. He is determined to live and we are determined too. We are not afraid of death – why should we be? If our belief system means anything, then we win with death anyway. However, we also believe that "whom God heals"[the meaning of Josiah] should overcome this, and there is purpose for him in life.

2 Cor 4:8 We are hard pressed on every side, but not crushed; perplexed, but not in despair;

The truth is that we are more than conquerors and able to make it through this time of stress. We will have a great story to tell at the end, but in the meantime we fight to win, not beating the air.

*1 Cor 9:24 Do you not know that in a race all the runners run,
but only one gets the prize? Run in such a way as to get the
prize. Therefore I do not run like a man running aimlessly; I
do not fight like a man beating the air.*

The facts change, but truth is unchangeable.

We are going to win.

Love

Steve

At no time did we ignore the facts about Rocky – but we did face
the truth.

God heals.

Sometimes we don't win battles, but it doesn't alter who God is.
I knew my son looked like he was dying, but I also knew it should
have been over months before. I knew that God had answered
prayers dynamically for me, for my family and for Rocky. All we
needed was one more.

My declaration to everyone was that we were going for an outright win. It wasn't enough to draw with cancer and losing was not
on our agenda. We fought for an outright win – a complete knockout
and we did so because we were being renewed inwardly.

*Therefore we do not give up; even though our outer person
is being destroyed, our inner person is being renewed day by
day. For our momentary light affliction is producing for us an
absolutely incomparable eternal weight of glory. So we do not
focus on what is seen, but on what is unseen; for what is seen
is temporary, but what is unseen is eternal.*

2 Cor 4:16-18 HCSB

We fought with this attitude, even though I had to administer his
morphine, coax him to eat, carry him, toilet him, watch his weight
falling and see his skin ever paler as his blood count dropped.

We resisted the *facts* because we were the people who really did
face up to the *truth*.

27 *Ups & Downs*

By the end of March 2001 Rocky's weight was critical and his food intake was tiny. On the last Sunday that month we made this a major issue of prayer during the church service.

One man in the church stood up and declared "Rocky has turned the corner". This was very encouraging. However an older gentleman stood up saying that he wished to confirm this by saying "Rocky has gone round the bend".

I couldn't help but laugh – especially as I wasn't sure whether it was Rocky or me who had gone round the bend!

I got home and Rocky was hungry. He said he could fancy a McDonalds Happy meal with chicken McNuggets. There was a drive through McDonalds about 5 miles away down the A64, so I set off like a shot. The road junction has been changed since, but at the time I had to take my life in my hands to cross the carriageway on the way home.

I got the meal home and he ate most of it. Later on he fancied more so I went back and bought another.

Over the next few weeks he fancied a lot of McNuggets and so I risked life and limb crossing the A64 a lot – but it was worth it just to see him eat.

That same week he suddenly said he could eat a KFC – so I rushed into town and bought him a two piece meal.

It is so funny – we have spent all our lives feeding our children healthy food and keeping them away from a high fat/sugar diet, but for Rocky it was just what he needed! If he had asked for a lard sandwich I would have dashed out to buy it!

Over 5 days he visibly put on weight and he felt so good that when some friends had a new kitchen fitted Rocky asked out of the blue if we would take him over to see it! The next thing we were in the car and he toddled around their new installation telling them it was very good but not quite as good as ours!

When we got home he was bushed but he did ask to make sure that I took him to church the next day.

The stewards used to leave us a space at the front of the car park and make sure we weren't blocked in so that we could leave at any time and be certain to get away as soon as we needed to.

On our 18th wedding anniversary (16th April) he woke up with a swelling around one eye. This reminded us of when he was first diagnosed and it wasn't a pretty sight. It hurt him when he blinked and a lot of the day he kept that eye closed. As we prayed over a couple of days it went down again.

Rocky's eating was erratic but still better than it had been. What made a dynamic change was when Sally from Candlelighters rang up and offered us a break at Bridlington. She had heard how Rocky was doing and wanted to give us the opportunity to take him away for a few days.

At the end of April Rocky not only wanted to go, but had a good journey and as soon as he could smell the sea air he asked to go to the doughnut shop. He sat eating doughnuts and then asked for chips. What joy!

He seemed to have more energy and a determination to do things that he wanted, like play the Star Wars machine in the arcades (winning all three missions), visiting the John Bull Rock factory, and eating his daily freshly fried donuts on the sea front.

He ate like a healthy boy, although we struggled getting enough fluids into him. What was really weird was that he started shedding skin almost in a reptilian fashion, which we put down to a lack of fluids. He had bowel movements in Bridlington without the aid of laxatives. This was a blessing on every level. We had been giving laxatives to Rocky but he knew what every pill was and could not be fooled. He didn't like taking laxatives because it made his stomach churn – so he would refuse. We used to play a few tricks to get them down him, because we needed to keep things going as much as possible.

Back home his appetite dropped again and he began to sleep for longer. One morning Pauline found a lump on his neck. It is impossible to express what it felt like to find this but we had to carry on the fight and continue to believe irrespective of any lump.

What no one could believe was that he was still alive and enjoying every day. He wasn't a whiny moaning child, nor did he just lay there lifeless. He was cramming as much in to each day as his energy would permit, and loving it all.

He loved to have visitors and to some he even gave a cuddle. He was very fond of a cuddle with our friend Paul, who would sit there with him for hours if that was what Rocky wanted. We had become used to it but he was a sweaty little boy – probably due to the cancer's activity in his body. Anyone who was blessed to have a sweaty cuddle enjoyed it, but the one that Rocky loved most was always with his Mum.

At the end of January, no one would have dreamed it possible, but Rocky was still going strong on May 8th – his 7th birthday. We decorated the house with banners and streamers. We decorated the outside of the house with a huge banner and even the trees in the front garden. No-one could come down the street without knowing that someone at number 20 was celebrating.

The postman delivered 43 birthday cards and from breakfast to bedtime visitors thronged the house. Another dozen cards were hand delivered.

King Josiah, his namesake, ascended to the throne when he was 8 years old. Could it be that Rocky would see another birthday? Our prayer was that he would and it was all I talked about that day.

Rocky was glued to his new Gameboy! (So I broke my no video games in the home rule!)

That day was so wonderful and even neighbours that we hadn't seen before entered into the spirit of the occasion.

By the beginning of June we had another opportunity to visit Bridlington courtesy of Candlelighters. Again the eating improved, a bowel movement took away all his energy though. We had a great time on the front at Bridlington and especially riding the little train. Rocky was painfully thin and needed to be well wrapped up even though it was not cold.

His morphine rose as high as 1.4g per day in two 700mg doses, but as June went on, his requirements fell day by day. By the time we got to June 26th any more than 360mg would have anaesthetised him. By remaining in control of his dose and monitoring him carefully to ensure he was in no pain we were able to avoid overdosing him into oblivion.

Our GP could not get his head round the falling dose of morphine, but he examined Rocky and confirmed he was in no pain. The hospital told me that no child needed less morphine as time went on; "It doesn't happen like that", was the quote.

Most of the time Rocky enjoyed the day. He didn't like taking laxatives, and he got a little grumpy occasionally. His inability to walk frustrated him and one afternoon, much to our shock, he became angry and shouted "I am just a useless piece of skin". Melody gave him a cuddle and we all rallied round. Very soon he was back in the swing of the day, but it reminded us that this really was a fight for Rocky and that he was fighting valiantly.

We all had our useless moments. It was a fight for us to stand under the constant pressure – but we had no choice. Battles are not won by those who lie down and die –only by those who fight on. Some days we stood from minute to minute, but we did continue to stand.

In June he had a mild chest infection which he had a course of antibiotics for. Our GP had to walk through doors that all had scriptural promises on them every week. When he saw Rocky, he told me that he really didn't understand why he was alive but maybe somewhere our faith was indeed giving us some sort of miracle.

No-one was denying the truth of what we saw, but this kind and professional GP was as amazed as we were and he was not going to rob us of our hope.

The chest infection further suppressed his appetite. He ate a single square of chocolate and vomited it straight back.

We knew no one who had experienced a miracle at this stage but miracles aren't based on statistics; all we needed was one. As I said to a work colleague on the phone who couldn't accept that miracles ever happened, "my life is full of positive statistical abnormalities". The joke was that he could accept that as long as I didn't use the word 'miracle'.

Earlier in the year the church had booked an American preacher, who had a ministry in praying for the sick and dying, to hold meetings in June. It was like putting candy in sight of a child but just out of reach. If only he could have come earlier. Except, of course, Rocky lived longer than anyone said he would!

So when the healing preacher arrived, Rocky went to church.

He was weak, couldn't walk and had to be carried in a blanket, but Rocky made it to church and was prayed for.

Afterwards Rocky slept peacefully like a baby and awoke refreshed and happy.

Now we would look for a result.

28 *Daddy & Rocky Day*

It was June 26th 2001.

Rocky seemed especially weak.

How much longer he could carry on being so thin and so pale we did not know.

Our GP couldn't understand how Rocky was still with us.

Ward 10 could not understand how Rocky was still with us.

We knew that our prayers were doing something.

The night before we had decided to go to Bridlington for the day. At least there we had some hope that Rocky would eat. We thought of those doughnuts and chips and looked at his fragile frame. He looked like something you saw on an Oxfam poster – except he was happy.

When we awoke, Rocky was in no hurry to get up. I told him that we were going to Bridlington and he said that he wasn't going, so I told Pauline to take the girls, as they were looking forward to it and we would take Rocky another day.

There was a moment of indecision, should she? Shouldn't she? But Pauline needed to get out of the house, and the girls deserved a day trip.

So my four blondes set off to Bridlington and I waited for Rocky to 'come round'.

Rocky didn't stay in bed. He always wanted to be in the living room with everyone else and it did seem strange that he was having a 'lie-in'. This was the latest start to a day we had experienced.

When he awoke, we sat together on the settee. He knew his sisters were in Bridlington but he said "today we have a Daddy and Rocky day" so we cuddled up on the sofa to enjoy each other's company.

He was very boney, but he loved a cuddle!

I asked Rocky what he wanted to do and he said "we will watch 2 movies – 1 of your choice and 1 of my choice". With that we sat down to watch 'Digimon' and 'Close encounters of the third kind' – I let him have his choice first.

At some point during our movie day, as I was trying to get him to eat something, we had a slight tête à tête. As I was coaxing him to eat I said, "but you have to eat something, Rocky!"He replied "I am not eating anything now – I AM NOT GOING TO DIE!"

After his loud protest, I returned to my comfy position on the sofa and didn't press the issue again for a couple of hours.

I will never forget Rocky telling me so emphatically that he wasn't going to die.

It was clear that Rocky had no fear of death. We had given him a clear understanding of life, death and heaven. We knew the importance of talking about such matters. I always felt so sorry for children whose parents ignored such things. Allowing Rocky to have his own relationship with Jesus was what he wanted and his decision. He wanted to carry on living and was fighting and praying to do that.

I don't know how many times we had watched 'Digimon' together, but that day we did it again. He did love watching 'Digimon' and 'Pokemon'.

The DVD collection had become important over these last couple of years. Many times it was the only thing that Rocky was well enough to do. I remember him going to the cinema to their Saturday morning Kids Club. He would love the movie, but he also loved the games at the end. These DVD's were our 'day out at the cinema' and he really loved it.

Rocky always thought it was important that if he got to choose a movie then someone else had to choose the next one. As there was only me there I got to choose, but I remember watching Rocky as much as Spielberg's masterpiece – I was trying to decide whether he really enjoyed it or whether he was just wanting me to enjoy it.

'Daddy and Rocky' day was a special intimate time, but like all of those days – we decided to make good memories, we decided to enjoy ourselves and we revelled in the love we had for each other.

It is amazing what a difference our own attitude makes to each day. Pauline and I helped each other so much on that front. 'Leadership' isn't often a word we use when thinking of families, but we have found and know that children are looking for good leadership from their parents. We lead our children all the time – but the question is how well do we lead them?

By the time we had watched two movies Rocky was ready for a rest.

Just in time, his mum and sisters returned home. Rocky said goodnight to them as I carried him to bed.

I remember how cold and clammy his skin felt next to me. If I breathe in I think I can just capture the scent of his sweaty body next to me. I took Rocky to bed and tidied up the kitchen.

Pauline and the girls arrived home – they had enjoyed a super day at Bridlington and we shared stories – me telling about my super cuddles with Rocky and our movie highlights and Pauline talking about their fun and her concerns about not being with our son. But for me, the joy had been having a Daddy and Rocky day!

Rocky had only had a short day, though. With all that was happening I can't say that we felt any more uneasy – every day was a challenge.

As our heads lay on adjacent pillows Pauline voiced the question that we were both thinking. 'How much longer can we go on like this?'

I prayed silently to Jesus and cried out "how long, Lord?" as I once again asked for my son to be healed.

I cannot really convey what the pressure felt like. The New Testament uses the word 'affliction' which literally means 'pressure'.

*we also rejoice in our afflictions, because we know that afflic-
tion produces endurance*

(Rom 5:3 HCSB)

It is very difficult to rejoice under pressure – but when we do it
enables us to endure. That night, like every night, I thanked God
that we had one more day together with our boy. Rocky loved his
mummy, but that day had been 'Daddy and Rocky day'. I was
grateful for our day together.

Like Pauline, I didn't know how much more pressure I could
take, but we had to make it through!

Endurance is one of the most profound words in the
Christian vocabulary. It is the one that I like the least, but necessary
all the same.

The great men of the Bible endured much. Paul says that

*we have commended ourselves in every way, with great endur-
ance, in persecutions, in difficulties, in distresses*

(2 Cor 6:4 NET)

He had to put up with a lot more than I did, so I figured I could
make it because we served the same God.

*Endurance produces proven character, and proven character
produces hope.*

(Rom 5:4 HCSB)

We knew that whatever the outcome of this great battle, our
characters were what mattered, that was what would be the testi-
mony of God's power. So we endured another day, finding that our
hope was still there – a living, breathing entity.

It has to be said that if Rocky could endure, then we had to as
well. What was going on inside his little body was a mystery, but he
was still enjoying life.

29 *The Day It Happened*

It was almost six in the morning. The next day had come quickly. As usual, I was woken by the cry "Father- toilet!" and I went downstairs to see to the needs of my son. As I was the morning person this was my routine, just as Pauline saw to him at night.

What was unusual that morning was that Pauline had followed me downstairs, and we saw to him together. Pauline had heard Rocky shout for her; I did not hear this call, neither had she heard Rocky call for me.

Rocky looked weak and frail, but he was very much our boy. I was going to put him back in his bed, but Pauline and I exchanged a glance and we decided to sit with him for a few moments on the settee.

Who can truly understand what passes between a man and a woman in a glance? We didn't need to discuss this; we were just going to spend a few minutes on the sofa. Pauline sat down, and I lowered Rocky into her lap. I sat down next to them and I held my son's hand.

He was thin, but so handsome.

Snuggled into his mum, whilst I held his hand he just slipped away. It was 6.10am and the battle seemed over.

We wept.

I cried out, "God, my son – my only son".

I heard a voice in the room say, "That's OK, I know that feeling too".

That was all I needed to hear from God.

I tried commanding his lifeless body to rise from the dead.

The room remained quiet except for the tears.

Pauline continued to hold him.

I rang the Doctor to tell him, and I rang our church leader.

Pauline said that I needed to tell the girls and ask if they wanted to hold him and say "goodbye". It was important that they were not afraid at this time.

I woke them and got them together in one room to tell them that their brother had died. I asked them if they wanted to hold him.

Two of them desperately wanted to hold him, but one preferred only to look and stood at the doorway for what seemed to be an age.

We all wept.

The doctor arrived. No-one could have been kinder or more thoughtful.

By half-past six he had checked Rocky and confirmed death.

His regular visits had meant that no autopsy was necessary. He wanted to save us from that trauma.

Pauline's sister Lynn was next to arrive; she was always there when it mattered.

Our church leader arrived and tried to be kind. He wasn't brilliant at times like this, but we were so pleased that he came. He asked what he could do for us that day and Pauline requested the removal of Rocky's bed – something which he came back later on the same day for and disposed of. This was a very important thing for Pauline – something I wouldn't have thought of, but part of the process of mourning is to be very sensitive to each other's needs.

Now what happens next? In a situation like this, what do you do? We knew that his death was a possibility, but he had lived exactly five months from being diagnosed in relapse. We had lived with him for over 7 years – almost 8 if you count the months we talked to him through the wall of Pauline's womb.

We had the offer of Martin House and use of the cool room. This was a place you could leave your dead child and come back and visit for a few days until the funeral. We both wanted to take him there.

Pauline said that she alone was going to prepare his body – wash him and dress him. Rocky looked serene, with skin that was almost like marble. Only God knew how low his red cell count had fallen in those last few weeks.

I thought carefully before doing this, but I took some photos of him. I am always glad that I did this.

We loaded the girls in the car and Pauline held Rocky as we drove to Boston Spa and took him into the cool room. The staff were respectful, sensitive and extremely helpful. We stayed a while, but then decided to tell Grandma and go and get her.

We went home and started announcing to the family the loss of our dear boy.

Lynn brought Pauline's mother. We all went back to Martin House to see Rocky. Grandma sat with him caressing his head and weeping. For Pauline and me, this was a moment of amazing clarity. We had left our boy in that cool room, but only when we returned did we realise it wasn't him.

Yes, he looked like Rocky, but something had changed – we used a phrase which we have said many times since. Rocky had moved house. He was no longer there. The body on the bed was a husk – empty of our son's essence. His eternal soul had moved on; he was with Jesus in paradise.

Rocky was to remain there for 3 days, but we knew at that moment that we would not return to view his husk again. Our son had moved on, and there was no longer anything relevant to look at.

What else happened that day? I had to find a funeral director and arrange an appointment. I had to speak to our church leader to arrange the funeral date too.

We had lots of tears on Wednesday June 27th 2001; an awful lot of tears.

But I had heard God say, "That's OK, I know that feeling too". For the first time in my life I think I truly understood how awful it was for God to see the dead body of Jesus. It would probably be more accurate to say that, for the first time, I was able to receive a particular comfort that passes between fathers who have been bereaved of their sons.

I don't remember going to bed, and I am not sure what sort of sleep I experienced. I felt like I had lived for months in a tumble drier. In a sense it was the stopping that was hard now.

We had lived with him for 7 years.

Now we had to learn to live without him.

That day I sent the following email to all those who had faithfully prayed for Rocky's healing:

> *Rocky went to be with Jesus at 6am this morning.*
>
> *It was a peaceful and precious time on his mother's knee with me touching his hand.*
>
> *God is good, we didn't expect this outcome, but we know that the fight was well fought. Right up to the end he wanted to live, but his body could not sustain him.*
>
> *Right now he is partying!*
>
> *Details of the funeral to follow when we have made arrangements.*
>
> *I am sorry to bear this news, but it doesn't change what we believe.*
>
> *Thanks to all of you for your prayers*
>
> *God bless you*
>
> *Steve*

I was right – it didn't change what we believed.

30 *The Day After*

The hardest thing about bereavement is learning to live without your loved one.

The day after Rocky died, what was so weird was that he wasn't there to experience any of what happened next.

The big plus for the bereaved in those first few days is the amount of time spent on preparing a funeral. It keeps the mind busy.

We didn't like the word funeral. We figured that this was just a big send-off for someone who had moved house. So we advertised the event as 'Rocky's Big Send-Off'.

We had been expecting to organise Rocky's wedding some day, and so we treated it more like a celebration. Pauline had been looking forward to cheering Rocky and his future bride down the aisle (a bit of a tradition in the church we were part of) and so her first request was that Rocky should arrive to cheering.

The funeral director was excellent. She was sensitive and helpful. We were glad of their service to us.

We picked a white coffin for Rocky and chose to have him cremated.

Some Christians don't like the idea of cremation, but we have always felt that a grave can be both a burden to maintain and an unnecessary shrine. We have no problem with other people's graves, but for us we felt it appropriate to not have that particular 'place'. We had long since decided that we would both be cremated when the time came.

We looked through our collection of home videos and found about three minutes of Rocky that we wanted to share with everyone. It included him singing *"When the moon hits your eye like a big pizza pie that's amore"*.

Looking at videos made us cry and laugh at the same time. We held each other and questioned how we would live without him. We both knew that whatever our experience the goodness of God was real and that Jesus would be with us. We would live – but we would deeply miss our little boy.

The hours were long that day and the tears were frequent.

We continued to support our girls. They were dealing with events in their own way, but we made sure they had extra cuddles during those days. We encouraged them with every good thing that we could find to encourage ourselves.

One thing that really helped us at the time was the way that Rocky remained handsome to his death. We had been warned that neuroblastoma often affects the face during relapse. I myself had seen examples of children who had been horribly disfigured by cancer before they died. We rejoiced that our little boy was still gorgeous to the end. It was a small thing – because it wouldn't have altered our love for him, but it was just a fact that we could take some comfort from.

We discovered throughout Rocky's illness that finding things to be grateful for was important to his attitude and ours too. We now applied this philosophy to ourselves.

We had stored many good memories during Rocky's journey. We now withdrew them from the memory bank – *with interest.*

The burden of events, the unpleasant end to our fight and the sheer shock of losing someone that we loved so much had taken their toll. We were stressed, exhausted and very vulnerable.

Two conflicting sets of feelings fought inside us. Our own need to mourn and to come to terms with the separation from our son fought with the ethos of the church that we belonged to that frowned on mourning. We had been taught that mourning was unnecessary and tantamount to personal failure. This close to Rocky's death, we were struggling to manage our emotions – the views of others were not entirely in the forefront of our minds.

To some degree, even at this time, we felt the pressure to conform, but to a great degree this day was according to our wishes. The real pressure was to come later.

We both felt that we needed to speak at our son's send off; so we started to string our thoughts together.

We started to get enquiries about flowers. In a throw-away comment Pauline said – "Don't bother with flowers – just buy me a new Dyson". Within a week people had donated enough for us to have our new vacuum cleaner. Pauline had explained to me that flowers would only last days but we could keep the house clean for years with a Dyson!

I was drawn to the story of David, fasting for his son with Bathsheba. When the boy died he stopped fasting and got up to refresh himself. When asked about his actions he responded this way:

"While the baby was alive, I fasted and wept because I thought, 'Who knows? The Lord may be gracious to me and let him live.' But now that he is dead, why should I fast? Can I bring him back again? I'll go to him, but he will never return to me."
2 Sam 12:22 HCSB

I realized that I also would go to Rocky, but irrespective of what I would prefer – he would not be coming back to me. This had been a long haul – we needed the closure of Rocky's big send off, but we also needed refreshment.

We prepared a montage of photos of Rocky with a simple message to give out as a souvenir of the event. A friend arranged for them to be printed for us.

We picked songs. We chose "The Blood shall never lose its power "(Andraé Crouch), "The Great Divide" (Point of Grace), and especially Rocky's favourite "I can go the distance" (Michael Bolton). The latter was from the Disney animation Hercules.

In Hercules, the young man discovers that he is actually the son of a god. Although he has the greatest muscles in the world he discovers that "a hero's strength is measured by his heart". This line became the centrepiece of the great song of the movie.

Children who have cancer, and face it well, will inevitably be called heroes. Rocky was a hero – it wasn't because of what he did, but who he was. These souvenir cards had this line from the song as their heading and then underneath "Rocky Josiah Redman went the distance from 8th May 1994 to 27th June 2001 and found a hero's welcome waiting for him at the end of his journey."

Rocky's big brave heart was that way because he knew Jesus. Jesus, the Son of God, arranges for all who call on His name to become adopted sons of God; Rocky was only a very little boy living with his mum and dad when he was adopted by a heavenly Father.

Hercules fictionally was a son of a god. Rocky in reality was a son of God.

He fought through his last 3 years of life with no intention of giving up, but sat on his mum's knee, holding his dad's hand, his little body could not continue any longer.

He ceased to be my responsibility and became entirely Father God's responsibility.

He will always be our little hero.

That day I sent the following email to our prayer list:

Subject: Last 28th June

Someone commented to me the other day, that they looked for the messages about Rocky with the subject line "Latest...". My weird sense of humour suggested that I send this message out under the subject "Last ."

It has been a substantial journey of nearly 2¾ years caring for Rocky in his fight for life, and the pilgrimage continues, for now we have to learn to live without someone who has been a major focus for so long. For Rocky, he has moved on to a hero's welcome, for us we will continue the journey, just as we have done. We know that it isn't over for us, and we will think we heard him shout or we will maybe just shed a tear here or there. We will keep soft hearts and apply God's principles to our lives, because we know that God is good.

We will not be conforming at his funeral but will give Rocky a good send off. Those of you on this mailing list who are able to attend, we would love to see, because you have stood with us at all times.

If you come along, then please do not wear black and receiving this mail means that you are invited back to the church after cremation to a small reception.

The funeral starts at 11.00am on Tuesday 3rd July. The cremation is at 12.30 also in York. For those of you who don't know where we are a map is attached.

God bless you all, we look forward to seeing many of you on Tuesday.

love and sincere thanks for all your support

Stephen & Pauline, Elizabeth, Melody & Arielle

This *was* in fact the last email I sent out to this group of the faithful.

31 *Rocky's Big Send Off*

When you are lying in bed, just exactly how do you get up, knowing that this is the day of your son's funeral?

Possibly the dream-like state that I was still in helped me. Perhaps Rocky hadn't died. Maybe I was waking from a bad dream. Any minute now he would run up those stairs and jump in-between us.

I was kidding myself.

I had to get up and face the day. My wife, my girls and the church were looking to me. I had to face this – however hard. This was now my journey, and I would have to go the distance.

The night we announced our engagement a woman in the church told Pauline and me "it's you against the world!" Despite the fact that she explained to Pauline how to wash and dry pullovers in the same breath, this advice now came back to my mind and I realised that whatever happened, my wife and I were joined together. We are one. We had to face what was coming and I had to be a man.

Getting ready that day was not easy, but we all looked our best.

Rocky's shell arrived at the church on time. About 430 people cheered him up the aisle as our celebration of his life started. In the congregation were members of the nursing and support team from Jimmy's, and even someone from Martin House hospice. Most of our families turned up, and most of the church too. My work colleagues supported me too – including the man who took advantage of a director for me!

On the coffin was a wreath made of all his favourite sweets – flumps, chup-a-chups, chews and jellies.

The singers had rehearsed the songs we asked for and they gave wonderful renditions that we loved.

Pauline and I both spoke about our little hero and the challenge of learning to live without him.

After we followed Rocky up the aisle, we began with the song that point of Grace made famous "The Great Divide".

Silence
Trying to fathom the distance
Looking out 'cross the canyon carved by my hands
God is gracious
Sin would still separate us
Were it not for the bridge His grace has made us
His love will carry me
There's a bridge to cross the great divide
A way was made to reach the other side
The mercy of the Father, cost His son His life
His love is deep, His love is wide
There's a cross to bridge the great divide
God is faithful
On my own I'm unable
He found me hopeless, alone and sent a Saviour
He's provided a path and promised to guide us
Safely past all the sin that would divide us
His love delivers me
The cross that cost my Lord His life
Has given me mine
There's a bridge to cross the great divide
There's a cross to bridge the great divide

(Grant Cunningham & Matt Huesmann)

It seemed appropriate at a time in which a great divide had opened up between us and our son that the gospel message should be sung in this way reminding us that God willingly paid with the life of His Son

We watched three minutes of video together on the big screen that we felt accurately depicted the real Rocky.

Then I rose to my feet. What I said was written out in full – I didn't need the notes, but I was capable of 'losing-it' at any second and they helped keep me on track. This made me realise that 'full notes' are important in highly emotional situations.

I spoke of how Rocky was a fighter and his name had been appropriate. I also said that when we came to the point of the fight against cancer we didn't have to find out about God and 'bolt-on' faith, but it was foundational to the way we lived our lives- it was already 'built-on'.

To great cheers Pauline was next up on her feet. She said how she was stood there today not because it was easy but for her girls of whom she was so proud. She spoke of how their maturity was beyond their years and that they had come through this with distinction. Boldly, Pauline declared that mourning was a personal thing and had to happen, but that she would not apologise for turning a funeral into a celebration because it was what she wanted and that was what mattered that day. The girls had been to her and asked was it still alright to smile. Pauline said how she had told them that it was alright to cry and to laugh and to express what was in their hearts at this time. There's no right or wrong way to grieve – only what is appropriate to you'.

The thing that dominated Pauline's thoughts was a TV advert that was running at the time for an ambulance chasing company which said "where there's blame there's a claim". Pauline said that she had decided that she would blame no one – especially God for what had happened to us, she recognised that bad things happen, but that years ago she had made a claim against God's plan of salvation and that would see her through the days to come.

Her bold declaration was that "when the questions come, especially in the dark moments of the night, I know that I live under the extravagance of God's love and grace. The most powerful things I know over these last 7 years of my boy's life are that Rocky really loved me, and that he knew that I really loved him. This is how liberating love is – it enables us to overcome in a situation that would normally overcome us. The days ahead of living without Rocky are incomprehensible, but we will face them as we have faced everyday so far, with gratitude that God is good and that his love surrounds us everyday".

Anything that was said before or afterwards in the service seemed to pale into irrelevance after the power of those words.

Another song we chose was the Andraé Crouch classic 'The Blood will never lose its power'

The blood that Jesus shed for me
Way back on Calvary
The blood that gives me strength from day to day
It will never lose its power

For it reaches to the highest mountain
And it flows to the lowest valley
The blood that gives me strength from day to day
It will never lose its power

It soothes my doubts and calms all my fears
And it dries all my tears
The blood that gives me strength from day to day
It will never lose its power

The timeless truth of these words used to make me cry before that day. Today, whenever I hear it, I still struggle to contain my tears.

The service went well, and we were grateful that so many turned up to see Rocky off.

The service finished with the singing of 'Go the Distance' by Alan Menken.

As this was sung a slide show of photos of Rocky from all of his seven years was seen, ending with a photo taken two weeks before his death.

The instrumentalists continued to play as Rocky's shell was carried down the aisle out of church.

The car took us to the crematorium. Many people followed. We saw his coffin go behind the curtains as they slid shut. The friend who had been my best man grabbed me and we sobbed together. That moment will last forever.

As we returned to church for the reception, a member of the congregation came up to me and asked whether we all had passports. I replied in the affirmative and he said "that's good because in a couple of days you are going to Cyprus". This kind man owned a house in Cyprus and wanted to send us there for a break.

We had to spend the next two days shopping for shorts and summer tops – and then there was the packing. Setting off was very difficult though; the problem was simple, we were going on a family holiday *without* Rocky for the first time.

We discovered quickly that a major problem we had ahead of us was the fact that we would go places that Rocky loved, *without him*. We would go to new and interesting places that we knew Rocky would have loved, but we would be *without him*. We would face anniversaries, birthdays, family celebrations, good times and bad times – but all *without him*.

We arrived in Cyprus to a heat wave. Temperatures were over forty degrees but all the arrangements went well. A relative of the house-owner collected us from the airport and drove us for an hour to the villa. We arranged for him to take us back at the appropriate time too.

We were not there for more than an hour or so though before the onslaught started.

The Greek Cypriots are very male focussed and love their sons. In the one week that we were there we must have had more than a dozen people stop us to complement us on the beauty of our three blonde daughters, and each one of them said something to the effect of *"three lovely daughters but no son?"*

When a week hasn't passed since the funeral you really don't want to be reminded that you have no son!

The trips out and the food were wonderful; so was the air conditioning in the villa – were it not for that I am sure none of would have slept.

Unfortunately, despite having plenty of sun screen, all of us got sunburnt on the first morning and had to stay out of the sun for the rest of the week. We are all fair and none of us are really any good in such a climate. The sun in a July Cyprus was not good for the Redmans, and a society obsessed with sons didn't help either.

We made a couple of good memories, like the boat trip out to the UN supervised border, and the excellent local restaurant that we loved. The people who sent us were very kind, but in reality it was probably too early for us to have travelled. It was too difficult to really enjoy it at that time, and certainly with that weather – but who knows? I am not sure that we would relish going to Cyprus again.

Coming back we had a post midnight flight which was delayed. That journey was horrific and took us a couple of days to get over – but we kept telling ourselves that we should just be grateful that someone wanted to bless us with a holiday.

When we got home from Cyprus we had to return our car – our wonderful family space wagon. It seemed like a punishment – we had lost our son, so they were taking the car off us too.

I also had to arrange to return to work. I decided that I would go back on September 1st.

I realised that I needed a few new white shirts for work, so I went up to a menswear shop to buy them. I took them home and washed them before wear. Two of them shrank and the other two didn't – clearly they were faulty, so I returned them to the shop. When the manager refused to just exchange them but insisted on just sending them away for examination I lost my cool and gave him a piece of my mind.

The problem with giving people a piece of your mind is that if you do it too often you are left with nothing for yourself. I didn't sleep that night. I tried to persuade myself that my behaviour was excusable for a man who had just lost his son, been sunburnt in Cyprus and had his car taken off him.

However, none of that was really acceptable, so when the shop opened the following morning I was there to apologise.

Better to eat humble pie than to end up mindless.

A couple of days later the manager rang me and asked me to call in to collect my new shirts. I went back to work in a new shirt and attempted to restart my career. I was the manager who just disappeared – twice. I was regarded as unreliable by head office, but still had friends locally who welcomed me back.

On my first day in harness I was stood talking to my line manager when a member of the customer service team came over and asked him to intervene with someone who was complaining that we hadn't fixed his computer. I could recognise the man as someone I had dealt with six months before. He was elderly but we had discovered pornographic photos on his computer featuring his 70 year old wife. These were not something to look at on a full stomach.

My line manager hesitated to intervene because he was briefing me on changes in the company, so I said 'leave this to me' and went over to the man. He ranted on to me that his computer was running slowly and that it had been in for two days and we hadn't sorted it out yet. I didn't mince my words, but told him that if his hard drive hadn't been filled to capacity by the disgusting pictures of his wife his computer wouldn't have been running slow! He talked about art to me and I talked about him exposing my staff to images they didn't want to see. I told him that 2 days wasn't a long time to wait and that he should get a life.

He calmed down and asked me where I had been. I bluntly told him that I had been nursing my seven year old son who had just died and that this was my first day back at work. I told him to get his life into perspective! He went out with his tail between his legs.

One hour later, flowers and chocolates were delivered to the store with an apology from the customer.

My line manager was suitably impressed. The story circulated around managers in the region and before I knew it I was shuttling around stores with the worst customer service problems. I was even given the project of sorting out the call centre when it was six weeks behind with complaints. I got it up to date in two weeks!

I am a gentle man, and don't like confrontation, but dealing with a few lost computer files is nothing like dealing with the loss of your son. My new realism helped a few customers and helped make a few good business decisions too.

32 *The Good Dream*

Whatever happened to the prophecies that Rocky would become an evangelist? How could Rocky tell people God's good news when dead?

It would just be easy to say that prophecy is not set in stone and that events can overtake it. After all, many of us have made bad decisions which have affected outcomes in our lives. We experience consequences to our actions and that surely impacts on prophecy, doesn't it? The weakened nature of man and the full force of cancer may have made a difference.

A broad understanding of Scripture leads me to the conclusion that cancer was never God's plan and I don't believe for one minute that the divine intention was for my son to suffer and die. It still happened though.

When we slip into the error of claiming that everything that happens is God's will, we make God out to be smaller than He is. By imagining a God who must decide everything in order to still have all authority and power we impose on God our own concept of what being omnipotent is. Whenever we impose our own understanding on God we diminish His greatness.

The real greatness of God is that in the beginning of all things He turned to Himself and said '*Let us make man in our image, in our likeness and let them rule*' (Gen 1:26 NIV). He is not so unsure of His own power that He can't share it. God is so comfortable in His own position and so confident in Himself that He made man in

His own image and gave him the right to rule. No one would deny that man has had an impact on the environment – poisoning rivers, filling the earth with rubbish and our atmosphere with particulates. It is not only the physical atmosphere that we have spoiled but the spiritual too. The impact we have had on our own health, wealth and inner wellbeing is related not so much to the will of God but the unrestrained, selfish and thoughtless will of man.

The Bible is clear that Adam and Eve rebelled against God contrary to His plan. Both testaments are full of the stories of flawed people who sometimes did what God asked and sometimes they did not. The promise that we have is that '*in all things God works for the good of those who love him, who have been called according to his purpose*' (Rom 8:28 NIV).

We were sustained throughout Rocky's fight and are still full of hope today because we believe that 'stuff happens but God is good'. Thank God we didn't start this fight with a belief system that everything happens because of the finger of God. I also thank God that we didn't allow our belief system to be changed because of what we experienced, but we continued to live in the revelation of Scripture.

I could also say that this was a case of a few 'bad' prophecies. Perhaps several people got it wrong. If we are honest there are a lot more dodgy prophecies out there than we would like. To base what we believe on a couple of prophecies alone is always questionable. Personally however, I do not believe they were wrong. God is not the author of confusion, but when there are times that we cannot see, we should wait and take time to listen to God.

I do have an answer to this question, and I am about to share it with you, but first let me tell you some of the things that have happened to me since Rocky's death.

I have spoken at a number of events on behalf of the wonderful charity Candlelighters that fights children's cancer. At the time of writing I am a trustee of the charity. Many times I have described the experience of having a child with cancer, and each time I have been able to share the reason for the joy and hope that is within me – because God is good and that walking through life with Jesus allows you to overcome all of its troubles.

On many occasions I have spoken to nurses in training at Leeds University and more recently at York too. I tell them our story, but it is so much a story of knowing God that he pops up everywhere. I always provide Kleenex.

I have been interviewed on local radio and national Christian magazines. Thousands of people that I normally would not have access to have heard about the goodness of God and the love of Jesus Christ because of Rocky. Hundreds of thousands have heard through our church website www.the-ark.net . The pages that tell his story are always popular on our web statistics and to this day we have people come to church because they have read about Rocky on the net.

Amazingly, he is still speaking to people!

A nurse who looked after Rocky once told me of a quandry she had found herself in. She was caring for a young man who was in relapse and knew that he was dying. He wanted to go home for his birthday and was stable, but she couldn't get hold of the consultant to authorize his 'day-out' of hospital. She told me that she sat in the office and asked herself what Rocky would do. She told me that Rocky inspired her to release the young man on her own authority.

He went home had a great day and made some videos of his family. Returning to hospital he worked from his bed to prepare some wonderful edited video memories for his family to keep after he died. He only lived a few more days.

The nurse was told off for releasing him without permission, but the boy and his family gained so much from her decision. It would appear that, in some way, the memories burned inside her head of a special little boy called Rocky were still influencing her to do the right thing.

Pauline had been doing brilliantly, but eleven years of home schooling was wearing on her and she needed a break. One day I realised that unless I acted the pressure would be too much so I rang our local secondary school and got the girls a place for the next term. Regrettably home schooling stopped, but Pauline had time to heal and get her teeth into something else.

The head of the school was expecting three girls who might know the names of flowers but were otherwise deficient both educationally and socially. She was very shocked to find that they were mature beyond their years and well ahead in their studies for their age. They have all gone on to be good students, and their social skills are all the better for having had their formative years at home.

Pauline saw this as an opportunity to do something she had always wanted – to go and get a degree. So returning to nursing in order to fund her passage through university, she applied to study English literature and Theatre Studies in York and started two weeks later!

I had been preparing to leave the retail environment and go start a fresh expression of church before Rocky was ill. In 2003, at the same time that Pauline started university, I was given a great opportunity to start something in York, and I took it. In September I handed in my notice and left retail at the end of October. Thus was born the Ark Church, and to this time I am employed as the full time minister there.

In September 2008 I had a dream. Like all healthy human beings I dream all the time, but this was not a normal dream.

I was with Rocky in a wonderful place. It was a marvellous reunion. I recognized him – he still looked as I remember. He was happy and he was excited to show me around. We walked and talked. His appearance was age seven, but his conversation was that of a mature man; his enthusiasm and care-free attitude was that of a child, though.

Giddily and with the delight that he always embraced life with, he showed me where he was living now. There were sights that have faded from my mind because they were too wonderful, and there were simple lights and colours that were overwhelming in the joy that they represented.

I realized that I was with Rocky in paradise.

Incidentally, I never saw a cherub, a harp or a cloud!

We talked and shared in the special and intimate way that parent and child do. It was great fun!

He explained to me that he wanted to show me around much earlier but he had been waiting for Father's permission, but it had only just been granted. I recognised that he was calling God 'Father' now, in just the same way as he used to call me.

Rocky told me that it would have been inappropriate and premature to show me around earlier.

We sat and drank something refreshing and life giving together. It was the experience that Starbucks would like to give but can't even come close to delivering. We seemed to be there ages, and each moment was a thrill. Whereas the length of the natural day tires us, the longer I was there the more alert I became.

Finally Rocky told me that I had to go back now. Our goodbye was simple and although it was clear that Rocky had appreciated the visit, I could also sense that my departure was not going to diminish him in any way. I began to feel emotion rising within me that I knew would result in me weeping. With that I awoke sobbing. It felt like I had been ripped out of a warm pleasant place into a cold harsh winter. I realised that there were no tears where Rocky was and my leaving had been a sudden thing to accommodate my weeping. It had been so real.

Have you ever woken from a dream sobbing? It is a strange experience. But as I sat there I made a few notes to preserve my memory. It was as a tremendously fulfilling experience and I thank God for the glimpse of glory that I had that night.

Why have a dream like this? What was it about and could it have been true?

I have no doubt that I was allowed a glimpse of my son and the contented state that he was in. I am also convinced that there was a timely element in it too. We had passed what I believe was the final milestone –living longer without our son than we had lived with him. It was at this time that I was ready to see him again. I don't think I will have that experience again, until I join him.

If there was anything I learned from this dream it was simply the urgency of the message of Jesus. Death is only around the corner. The second coming of Jesus could be at any time. This age is drawing to a close, and the need for people to make their own connection with God through Jesus is desperate. This dream brought me comfort and a glimpse of glory – but most of all it reminded me of the purpose of the Christian life – to lead others to the Saviour.

What happened to Rocky being an evangelist? As long as he inspires me to communicate God's good news, and continues to open doors for me share the life of God with ordinary people, then he is fulfilling prophecy.

The Bible says of Abel who was killed by his brother Cain that:

"even though he is dead, he still speaks"

(Heb 11:4 HCSB)

God comforted me with this scripture and the realization that some ministries can still be completed posthumously. When you invite me to speak, read what I write or listen to me in cyberspace, my son is fulfilling his ministry to you.

33 *Milestones*

The journey through bereavement certainly has its milestones: the first time you go to a place without your loved one, the first time you go anywhere they would have enjoyed. When you watch a movie that they loved or see a person that they liked, it is a 'first'.

Birthdays, Christmas and anniversaries are particularly poignant.

It was impossible for me to look in Toys R Us without finding something for Rocky. This seemed very silly to me, but I was selecting toys that I wasn't going to buy for a child who was no longer alive.

I actually went as far as buying the next Pokémon movie on DVD because I knew that Rocky would have wanted it so we watched it together in remembrance. (Not that any of us even enjoyed Pokémon!)

When a new Star Wars movie came out we had to go watch it 'for Rocky'.

The way people deal with bereavement can sometimes look bizarre, but I have a lot of sympathy now.

What did we throw away? His clothes, his toys, his knick-knacks? To begin with we didn't throw anything away. Slowly we gave away a lot of his toys to other little boys, but we held on to a few items that he was particularly fond of. His big bear was to stay, his snake and his badger are still with us. His Star Wars figures and his Jar-Jar Binks back-pack remain to this day.

The hardest thing was his clothes. Certain items seemed to have his scent on them and from time to time either Pauline or I could be caught just holding a fleece or a jumper to catch the scent of the boy who moved house. One day, several years later, I foolishly moved some clothes from a cupboard into a plastic box in the loft. I disturbed something that Pauline was not ready to see moved. It took me a long while to forgive myself for that.

Going to Bridlington for the first time without him was especially hard. We went to the same donut shop that he liked and bought ice cream where he had. We also played on the same Star Wars arcade machine that he loved. It took us a year to get to the point where we were ready to spread his ashes – and we took those to Bridlington. We scattered them in the harbour and made the mistake of not checking the way the wind was blowing – we ended up covered in bits of our boy. We laughed at this, because we knew it would have tickled Rocky. None of us felt dirty or defiled by the dust – in some ways it seemed appropriate.

Going to London without him was hard – but to celebrate him we went back to Planet Hollywood and had a feast. The staff were still friendly and the fruit cocktails were still excellent. All the time we sat there tears were never far away. It probably meant nothing to them but we felt that we had to write to the manager and staff thanking them for the wonderful service we had with our boy and then without him too.

When we went to France, it was difficult because Rocky had never been there and we knew he would have loved it.

Christmas was such a big event in our household that when we got there without him it lacked something. Our Christmas routine is that we get up for church, then come home, open our presents and have lunch. Everyone has to wait and watch whilst each present is opened in turn. As a rule we start with the youngest and then take a turn each. Arielle had the first turn again, just as she did before Rocky came along. We had some marvellous Christmases with Rocky and we have had some great ones since, but we can't get through the day without remembering him.

A new Christmas tradition for us has been to open a bottle of bubbly on Christmas Day and toast Rocky as we sit down to our lunch.

The first birthday without him was the hardest, but each one that passes we realise that we can no longer imagine what he would have looked like. The milestones came thick and fast the first year and without doubt the second year was a little easier, because there wasn't one date on the calendar that we hadn't already experienced without him.

For the first three anniversaries of his death we arranged big fund raising evenings for Candlelighters. A couple of casino nights and a big band night all got us out of the house on a key day and helped us convert what could have been a sad night-in to a productive night-out. Each night produced a few thousand pounds for the charity.

The first one of these nights had all its printing provided free by Chris, a local printer. I gave him some photos to use for the posters and as a gesture he printed me out a one metre high laminated photo of my boy as a souvenir of the night. This larger than life photo adorns our hallway today and enriches our lives so much.

We were particularly happy when the Candlelighters laboratory developed a test for neuroblastoma – remember how the consultant told me that she thought they had got rid of the disease? No one ever has to think anymore – the test shows if the disease is still present. All the fundraising for this fabulous charity is worth it.

A major milestone was going back onto the ward to visit other parents. I spoke to the ward sister to ask her opinion as to whether it was appropriate, and she thought it would be useful. I started bringing cake onto the ward each Thursday afternoon and making coffee for the parents and giving them a place to sound off whilst eating something sweet.

The hero's board in Ward 10 always carried a lot of photos of children who had been treated on the ward. From time to time a nurse would 'edit' the board removing pictures of children who had relapsed and died. The board is a big help, because as you walk up and down the corridor you cannot help but see children who have survived and you have the ambition of getting your child's picture up there.

Over a year after Rocky died I walked back onto the ward to find my son staring down at me from the hero's board. After a while I picked up courage to ask Jolly why Rocky was still there and she told me that she just couldn't bring herself to take him down. As I write this, Rocky is still up on the board and every time I walk into the unit the first thing I do is check that he is still there; I don't think anyone else knows, but it means a lot to me.

Milestones continue, but I wonder if we have now passed the last significant one? Just before Rocky died he was seven years old. It was deeply significant when we passed the milestone of living longer without him than we did with him. Somehow, it was passing this particular milestone that really loosened my typing fingers to produce this book.

Only a few weeks after Rocky's death, I attended a church barbeque. There was a man there stood alone that I didn't know and so I approached him to find out who he was.

He was a Pastor from Zimbabwe and he told me that he was visiting his wife here in York. I don't know about you but I can't stand it when people tell me a story that has a mystery attached. Why would a man's wife live on a different continent?

With a few more questions I managed to extract the rest of the story. As a family they had very little money. At the time inflation was running at 160% in Zimbabwe (it rose a lot higher) and his wife had moved to England to work and send money back home. She was a trained nurse. The Pastor told me that in Harare where he ministered at least a third of the adult population were HIV+.

I asked him how he filled his time, and he told me that all he did was bury the dead and comfort the bereaved. From morning to dusk people were dying of AIDS and he had no time for any other activity.

I may not have known him, but he knew me. He gave me condolences on the loss of Rocky. I asked him what the average family size was in Zimbabwe. Ten or eleven was the norm, but only half would be raised to adulthood due to sickness. This man had passed many gravestones of children as milestones on his journey. Had we lived in Zimbabwe, maybe we would have lost more than one child.

Not every milestone we have faced over these years has been about Rocky, though his shadow has fallen on most of them. The thing about milestones is that you only pass them on your journey. We haven't stayed where we were – we have moved on. The milestones we pass are evidence of this. We aren't travelling in circles, in fact we move from one new adventure to another. I haven't been this way before, but then that is what adventure is all about.

34 *Happy Ever After?*

Bereavement hurts.

Loss is an intense feeling.

Sometimes people who are bereaved will ask me 'do you ever forget the pain?'

I guess this is the $64000 question.

If Jesus is the centre of your life and through self-discipline you maintain your relationship with God, then you will always gravitate to Him. When loss becomes an obsession, or a mesmerising well that we keep staring into, then we risk falling down a hole from which escape is difficult.

Tears are a natural process and feeling the separation is something that even the Father did as Jesus died on the cross. There is a time to mourn (Ecc 3:4) and we also read that we should '*rejoice with those who rejoice; mourn with those who mourn*' (Rom 12:15 NIV)

'A time to mourn' by implication tells us that there must be a time to stop mourning.

In the Psalms we read of a fascinating place called Baca, or 'tears'. As you will know from the trickles that have occasionally fallen down your cheeks, tears are salty. Fresh water teams with life, but salt water is ultimately a killer. Men adrift at sea will die of thirst though surrounded by water, because there they cannot live on salt water.

The scripture gives us three great truths about the valley of tears.

"As they pass through the Valley of Baca, they make it a source of spring water; even the autumn rain will cover it with blessings. They go from strength to strength; each appears before God in Zion."

(Ps 84:6-7 HCSB)

Firstly the valley of tears is a place to pass through. It is not a place where you build a bungalow! The valley of tears is on our journey, we have to go that way, but we must pass through and beyond it. It is inevitable that we are exposed to its environment, but if we are wise we will not book a restaurant there or buy any real estate.

In 1 Kings 13 we read the story of a prophet who God tells not to eat or drink anything in a particular place. Another man tells him that God has instructed him to go back with him to feast. The prophet allows himself to be deceived and, as a result of his disobedience, he is killed by a lion.

The prophet did the job he was called to but took his sustenance in the place he should not have. We have to shed tears, but we mustn't make it our life's work.

Secondly, when we stay drinking in the valley of tears we consume salty water that can kill us. If instead we travel through Baca with Jesus He will transmute our tears into springs of water. The one who turned water into wine can also desalinate our tears. The sting comes out of mourning and we are not diminished by the experience of loss.

We must take in life from the one who plants a spring of living water within us and not absorb the ache and pain of life that we experience along the way.

Lastly we see that those who travel through the valley finding the source of spring water go from strength to strength. What we initially see as loss, feels like loss and leaves an emptiness within us, will, if we allow God, become a strengthening process within us.

"Blessed be the God and Father of our Lord Jesus Christ, the Father of mercies and the God of all comfort. He comforts us in all our affliction, so that we may be able to comfort those who are in any kind of affliction, through the comfort we ourselves receive from God. For as the sufferings of Christ overflow to us, so our comfort overflows through Christ."

(2 Cor 1:3-5 HCSB)

In our afflictions or pressures, God comforts us. Knowing what we have been through and understanding it, He sustains us with a comfort that we can then recycle to others in their time of need. Our comfort overflows and we are strengthened in the process.

The valley of tears is real – but it can result in a stronger person. Don't lie there in the muck and mess soaking up every negative vibe that you can, but have your time of mourning, then move on and make it your mission to comfort others.

As I complete this book we have lived 8 years without our boy. I think of him every day. I miss him. I still have moments where I sit and shed a tear. Instead of being overcome with grief, I have overcome grief with the comfort God gives me. Rocky will not come back to me, but I will go to him. In the meantime, life is enriched in beauty and opportunity because of the comfort of God.

Recently I had to speak at the funeral of a young man who had committed suicide. It was a couple of days after the 8th anniversary of Rocky's death.

As I prepared myself, sat in front of my computer, my peripheral vision picked up a card that was stuck up awkwardly out of a pile. I reached to press it down but it would not move, so I pulled it up to realize it was a souvenir card from Rocky's big send off.

As I saw the message 'a hero's strength is measured by his heart', it occurred to me that it had been a long time since I heard the song. So I found Michael Bolton singing 'I can go the distance' on YouTube and also on the other side of my screen Googled up the lyrics to the song.

I have often dreamed, of a far off place
Where a hero's welcome would be waiting for me
Where the crowds will cheer, when they see my face
And a voice keeps saying, this is where I'm meant to be
I'll be there someday, I can go the distance
I will find my way, if I can be strong
I know every mile, will be worth my while
When I go the distance, I'll be right where I belong

Down an unknown road, to embrace my fate
Though that road may wander, it will lead me to you
And a thousand years, would be worth the wait
It might take a lifetime, but somehow I'll see it through

And I won't look back, I can go the distance
And I'll stay on track, no, I won't accept defeat
It's an uphill slope, but I won't lose hope
Till I go the distance, and my journey is complete

But to look beyond the glory is the hardest part
For a hero's strength is measured by his heart

Like a shooting star, I will go the distance
I will search the world, I will face its harms
I don't care how far, I can go the distance
Till I find my hero's welcome, waiting in your arms
I will search the world, I will face its harms
Till I find my hero's welcome, waiting in your arms

(By Alan Menken)

As I listened and read, I sobbed.

As the song ended, I blew my nose and shed the last couple of tears that I could find. My voice was squeaky and weak, but my heart was prepared for the funeral. At that moment the office phone rang.

There was no way that I was going to pick up that phone, but I looked through my teary eyes and saw that the phone number was not one I recognized and it was not local. Realising that I should push beyond my feelings about how my voice might sound I picked up the handset.

What followed was a conversation with a woman who needed prayer and was struggling with issues that were directly addressed by the lyrics of the song. She told me that she couldn't go any further down the road, that she had lost hope and her strength.

I read the lyrics to her and she cried. She told me I must think her silly for crying over the lyrics of a song. I came clean and told her that I had been crying over them when she rang.

We talked, we prayed.

When the conversation finished I laughed!

Of all the Pastors in the entire world this woman had rung maybe the only one who could speak into her need at that time.

Even the current tears are not without value.

I have one profound answer to the question 'do you ever forget the pain?'

I have chosen not to forget.

The most inscrutable problem that God ever encounters, the most difficult situation God has to deal with, the greatest challenge God faces is surely a hard heart. When we allow our hearts to become hardened by our reactions to life's pressures we make it difficult to connect to God and to our fellow man.

Sometimes we face this challenge – will I allow what I am experiencing to soften me or harden me?

On a recent trip to an ancient abbey, I discovered that the monks had collected their own urine to use in their tannery. The leather was softened by their own pee!

Something that we would seek to dispose of, turn our backs on and leave behind, can actually soften that which would otherwise be harder to work with.

I have chosen not to forget because it helps me maintain a soft heart.

Jesus Christ, Son of God and Lord of all in all of his glory acting in his heavenly ministry of high priest, is still now able to sympathize with our weaknesses (Heb 4:15 HCSB). If Jesus has not hardened His heart to what He felt as He walked the earth and was tortured to death, then there is value in not forgetting the modest pain I have felt.

I do not live in the place of pain any longer – but I do remember what it felt like. This way I am more sensitive to others and to God.

God feels.

He felt when He shouted in Eden "Where are you?" and He felt when He burst into this world to rescue us as a baby. He felt when He had compassion on the sick and the bereaved. He felt as they whipped Him, and nailed Him to a cross. As He struggled to breathe and His life blood trickled out of His body, He felt it all.

When we fail Him, He feels that too. When we hurt, He is moved.

The God that I know has felt it all and is able to stay with me, comforting me all the way.

We all feel different things as our experiences of life vary and our pilgrimage takes us different ways. I am convinced of this – that if we collect comfort on our way and remain sensitive, not forgetting the pain, then we are more useful to those we connect with. Also, as God feels our pain too, we connect more easily with Him if we keep our hearts soft.

Next time you feel that life has just urinated all over you (notice how polite my language is), let it soften your hide and find the comfort. Accept and process the comfort, then store it because you can be sure that elsewhere on your journey you will find someone bleeding and dying on the roadside who is waiting for a kindly stranger to pour in oil and wine. (Luke 10:29-37)

Does the pain ever go away? Not if you harness it and use it to good effect.

People often say to me 'it is alright for you!' Of course they are right – it is alright for me! If you believe as I do and look for every good and perfect gift that comes down from Father God then it will be alright for you too!

35 Patterns and Portents

I am convinced that people look for patterns in everything.

Some patterns are comforting, some are disturbing but all give some sense of order in the universe.

We can choose to relax in the knowledge that God can see the end from the beginning and that by faith in Him He will even work our trouble out for a blessing. Alternatively we can look for other mysteries in the patterns of our lives and worry that there is some hidden meaning.

My father died when I was seven years old.

When my son was seven years old, he died.

Are these two events connected? It is bizarre, isn't it?

Were my family cursed? These circumstances would be interpreted by some as indicating that we were out of the blessing of God.

Sadly, I have met those who measure the blessing of God by outward success. New cars, big houses and children with perfect teeth must indicate that God is with you!

By this measure Paul the apostle was clearly a man most cursed.

"Five times I received from the Jews the forty lashes minus one.

Three times I was beaten with rods, once I was stoned, three times I was shipwrecked, I spent a night and a day in the open sea,

I have been constantly on the move. I have been in danger from rivers, in danger from bandits, in danger from my own countrymen, in danger from Gentiles; in danger in the city, in danger in the country, in danger at sea; and in danger from false brothers.

I have laboured and toiled and have often gone without sleep; I have known hunger and thirst and have often gone without food; I have been cold and naked.

Besides everything else, I face daily the pressure of my concern for all the churches."

(2 Cor 11:24-28 HCSB)

I am sure that you will agree with me that contrary to circumstantial evidence, Paul was indeed a man most blessed!

So am I!

In fact when it comes to trouble, I can go head to head with anyone of you trading stories and comparing heartaches. *'Nobody knows the trouble I've seen, nobody knows but Jesus'*, but instead of talking about my troubles I choose to talk about my deliverances. I choose to rejoice in the many blessings I have received. We are a happy family, a together family and we have much to rejoice about.

My circumstances say nothing about me; how I respond to my circumstances says *everything* about me.

Many years ago Dwight Latham and Moe Jaffe wrote a comedy song. It is said that it was inspired by a paragraph written by Mark Twain purporting that a man could become his own grandfather.

Many, many years ago when I was twenty three,
I got married to a widow who was pretty as could be.
This widow had a grown-up daughter
Who had hair of red.
My father fell in love with her,
And soon the two were wed.

This made my dad my son-in-law
And changed my very life.
My daughter was my mother,
For she was my father's wife.

To complicate the matters worse,
Although it brought me joy,
I soon became the father
Of a bouncing baby boy.

My little baby then became
A brother-in-law to dad.
And so became my uncle,
Though it made me very sad.

For if he was my uncle,
Then that also made him brother
To the widow's grown-up daughter
Who, of course, was my step-mother.

Father's wife then had a son,
Who kept them on the run.
And he became my grandson,
For he was my daughter's son.

My wife is now my mother's mother
And it makes me blue.
Because, although she is my wife,
She's my grandmother, too.

If my wife is my grandmother,
Then I am her grandchild.
And every time I think of it,
It simply drives me wild.

For now I have become
The strangest case you ever saw.
As the husband of my grandmother,
I am my own grandpa!

We all know that because author has omitted the word 'step' in this song the conclusion is invalid. No-one can actually be their own grandfather. Yet, we look in the complexity of human existence for patterns to explain what has happened as if we were an ancient examining the intestines of a goat.

The reality is that when we miss out a single 'step' we misinterpret events and assign them meanings that they do not have. Our inability to fully comprehend God's big picture will always mean that we miss out one 'step'. The troubles of life only serve to reinforce the truth that we need a saviour to walk with.

Instead of looking for patterns, our time would be better spent examining God's book for truth and allowing time to commune with and listen to God. The challenge of troubles and pressures is to take the next step with Jesus.

I have been greatly comforted by Psalm 119v5: *Your word is a lamp for my feet and a light on my path*(HCSB). If we make God the centre of our lives then His Word will shine enough light around our feet that we can see the next step. We are not guaranteed to be able to see two steps ahead, but then when we take the one step, the next becomes visible anyway.

One step at a time is all we need to take.

So I know that I am blessed and not cursed, I know that the age that I was when my father died and the age that my son was when he died are barely relevant, and only one of those confusing patterns that I have seen in the randomness of cosmic events.

I also know that I am loved by a wonderful woman called Pauline, three fabulous girls called Elizabeth, Melody and Arielle, and by a God who never wanted any harm to come my way.

Recognising the love is the only pattern that really matters.

36 *Stepping Over*

In 1990 I was privileged to entertain Astronaut General Charles Duke for dinner.

Most of us remember his voice – but we don't realise because we were focussed on who he was talking to. Charlie was the voice at the earth side talking down Neil Armstrong as they descended to the lunar surface in Apollo 11. When Armstrong said "Tranquillity base here The Eagle has landed", it was Charlie who responded "you've got a bunch of guys here about to turn blue – we're breathing again". More importantly for him, it was Charlie who walked on the moon himself in Apollo 16.

When Apollo was on the go I was only a boy and absolutely gripped by the excitement of spaceflight. To later talk to a man who had walked on the moon was an ambition fulfilled. I listened to his story and found that he had come back from the moon with all his ambitions fulfilled only to find a great emptiness. After buying a brewery and getting no joy out of that, Charlie found Jesus.

He used to go around talking about his lunar expedition and saying "the excitement and satisfaction of walking on the moon doesn't begin to compare with my walk with Jesus that lasts forever. Not everyone has the opportunity to walk on the moon – but everyone has the opportunity to walk with the Son. It cost billions of dollars to send someone to the moon but walking with Jesus is free."

Those words are inspiring, but it was something he said across the table to me that stuck with me more than anything else. He often prayed for the sick and he was challenged once by someone who asked him "What would you do if you were praying for someone and despite all your prayers they dropped dead in front of you?" His response has never left me "I would step over their corpse and pray for the next one", he said, "because God heals".

As a Bible believing, born again Christian preacher and these days a full time Pastor too, I have to confess that losing Rocky hit me on many levels.

I couldn't imagine life without him.

I couldn't imagine how my wife would live without him.

I couldn't quite see myself praying for the sick without him.

What I can say is that I never questioned God – because those words that He said to me when Rocky died were enough. Many people live with a lama – not the woolly mountain animal – that would be llama. Lama is the word that Jesus spoke on the cross when he cried out 'eloi eloi lama sabachthani' – my God, my God WHY have you forsaken me? In a moment of being separated from the rest of the trinity – cut off from God by the stench and horror of the cross, Jesus cried out 'WHY?'

I am convinced that Jesus knew what was happening; after all He had been party to the great plan to save mankind. It was Jesus who had stepped forward and said 'send me'. Jesus realised that sin and its consequences were being dealt with in his body as an eternal sacrifice.

Jesus was just not prepared for the feeling of being cut off from God. This is a feeling all mankind knows, and one that it was necessary for Jesus to feel so that he truly had suffered in every way that a man can.

I wasn't asking myself *why* had this happened – only *how* can I carry on?

Understanding that "my circumstances say nothing about me; how I respond to my circumstances says *everything* about me" was not enough. I also needed to remember that my circumstances say nothing about God, and when they change God doesn't. My circumstances only serve as a vehicle in which to journey through life with Jesus, receiving and sharing comfort.

Understanding that Rocky's death said nothing about the love or grace of God to me and my family, nor of His blessing on our lives enabled me to do what I knew was such an important thing all those years ago when I heard Charlie Duke say it.

I stepped over Rocky's body and began to pray for the sick again.

I had always known that those words were significant, and never forgot them. I never dreamed that the body I would have to step over would be that of my son.

Our attitude to life is a critical component to our success. Stupid, mindless positive thinking may seem to have merits, but doesn't actually deliver the goods. Having the attitude that my wife inspired in me throughout our battle makes all the difference – at least it's not raining!

Someone asked me what would Pauline have said if it was raining that day? Frankly – that is a good question! However, it is very easily answered – somehow she would have found one thing in our living horror that we could be grateful for – maybe it would have been 'at least it's not snowing'.

She would have found that one thing to latch onto because she is that kind of woman – her attitude is good and she knows what really matters.

Through casual observation, sometimes people make the error of assuming I am just a positive kind of guy – it isn't an inner ability or a genetic trait, it is a choice I make daily to look for something to be grateful for.

Without the experience of meeting Jesus, I don't think I could have walked this journey without becoming damaged. Today, I am the happiest person you could wish to meet. I am happy because I have chosen to be. I am fulfilled because I am grateful, I am grateful because Jesus is my real saviour and His Spirit my constant companion.

I have none of the trappings that this world uses to measure success – not even a son! But I have the best wife, three stunning daughters and peace with God.

Life is a real roller-coaster ride, but…at least it's not raining.

37 *Afterword*

In 2003 I started building an Ark.

I always thought that one day I would find some nice pastor who was retiring or who was called to missionary work in some far flung part of the globe and replace him as leader of his healthy 300 strong congregation with its superb edifice and excellent remuneration package.

In 2003 I planted a new church on a slightly dodgy housing estate in York with no visible means of support . Translating that into English, I had no salary, no savings and no congregation.

I must have been nuts.

Or maybe that prophecy in Little Rock, and those encounters with God in Tulsa and St Louis, actually amounted to something?

I knew no one, I had nothing and no tangible resources to call on, but I knew I had to do it.

I trusted God , left my well paid job and we are still here. The contemporary Ark Church is now a feature on the Christian scene in historic York. I am well known in the city and the region as a leader, preacher and as Rocky's Dad.

As part of One Voice, a great Christian network of leaders in the city that still carries the charismatic heritage of the great David Watson, I have a voice amongst my peers and genuine friends across the churches.

As part of the wonderful network of Ground Level churches in the UK, I have relationships that reach beyond even the great nation of Yorkshire.

Through our website www.the-ark.net I have preached to thousands and my daily inspirational notes are read by tens of thousands of people a month.

My various connections through the community and through local media have put our story in the faces of many who would not normally take an interest in the words of a preacher like me. I am still involved with the children's cancer unit and the Candlelighters Charity, now as a Trustee.

The joy of working full-time for my heavenly employer is hard to put into words. The pressures that I deal with as a Pastor are not inconsiderable, and the financial issues of starting from scratch have not been insignificant. However God is good and the pressures of all of this have not been like fighting for your son's life *or seeing him die*.

Prophecy has certainly come to pass.

Did I hear you say "rugby"?

Is that a little jibe I hear from you, or is it perhaps a genuine expression of confusion? Are you one of those kind hearted folk who find annoying holes in other people's arguments and take pleasure in pointing them out?

I did put it in the book – I could have left it out.

Whatever happened about Rocky growing up to play rugby?

Good question. Thanks for reading the book. THE END.

I guess I have to address this, and actually it is not a big deal. It is easy to get really messed up about prophecies that don't come to pass, but DON'T DO IT!

I prophecy a lot. I am not infallible. That prophet in Arkansas isn't either. His batting average is great, but he isn't perfect.

To be honest that prophecy was a really good encouragement that helped us fight a good fight. In fact Rocky and the rest of us put up one hell of a good fight; I think hell was really frightened at times.

If all that word did was encourage us to fight, then it did its work.

We would love prophecy to be infallible, life to be predictable and to have a working theology that didn't have any creaking doors or holes in the back. What works best is just to admit things didn't work out and 'eat the meat and spit the bones out'.

Pauline sometimes like to tell the rest of us at the start of the film how it will end. Unlike most prophets my wife is always right – it is incredibly annoying!

The truth is that when we step outside the cinema into real life, we do not know how things are going to work out. We might see a pattern and think we know what is coming next, but we make choices, choices make consequences and consequences bite us on the bum. (I probably could have worked the phrase 'and points make prizes' into that sentence if I had wanted to).

Jonah prophesied that Nineveh would be destroyed, but people repented and God relented.

After all, rugby is only a game.

I once prophesied in a room of a dozen people, with only two women of childbearing age, that one of them would have a son in about a year and that they were to call him 'Simon' because *God had heard* them. When I got home I was nearly wetting myself with fear, because someone in that room had to be pregnant within a year, or I was going to look like a false prophet! I looked up the meaning of Simon, only to find it means 'he has heard'. I was so blown over by that fact, of which I had no previous knowledge, that I stayed full of faith all year. Just before the time was up one of those two women began to put on weight. Sure enough she had a son and she called him…*something else.*

Was I wrong? No – they just didn't like the name, or didn't want to admit that God had spoken to them.

When I went back and listened to the taped prophecy again, the 'man who told me everything I ever did' really struggled when he began to prophecy about Rocky and said something like "all I can see about your son is something about playing your British game rugby".

With hindsight he was struggling to find anything to say about him. Maybe the rugby bit was just a bit of a tangent, maybe his mind filled in a blank? Maybe he just screwed-up? Maybe we just needed something to hold onto on those long terrible nights?

Life is a very inexact science, and prophecy is no different.

If we can admit this and move on, we don't really have a problem. When we get all religious and honour the prophet out of all proportion, we are on very dodgy ground.

If Johny in Little Rock were to prophesy to me today I would listen attentively, with great anticipation. I have no problem about that elliptical ball in connection with my son's life. I have yet to meet anyone who has such a profoundly developed prophetic gift, but he had no delusions of grandeur – and I have no illusions about him or his gift either.

I have seen prophecy used as a manipulative tool. I have heard prophecies that could slice through steel and others that couldn't give you a paper cut. I have also seen it wonderfully build up the church and bring great blessing to people.

If I have anything in my life that has seen me through pressure, loss and pain, it has surely been the reality of my personal relationship with God through Jesus. It has *not* been prophecy. We must avoid an immature over-reliance on prophecy. It is an important gift in the church, but nothing trumps your personal relationship with God.

When I was a young man in church and wanted to talk things over with my Pastor, I would take 'big issues' to him only to face the same two questions. "What's your prayer life like, Stephen? When did you last read your Bible?" That man used to irritate me – he never prophesied over me or gave me any answers. He just wanted to know about my relationship with God – and that wasn't what I thought my problem was.

What has kept me sane and happy these many years is that I talk to God and He talks to me. I don't have a religious belief; I have a relationship with a God who loves me. I keep my marriage alive by working on my relationship with Pauline, and I keep myself alive by working on my relationship with Jesus. When a prophet speaks its greatest value is to confirm what I have already heard from God and to encourage me.

One prophecy that didn't work out does not affect my relationship with Jesus.

We should be open about prophecies that don't work out. If we have a sound New Testament attitude to prophecy rather than some over-hyped, personality-cult driven dependence on the words of some guy, then we won't stumble over this wonderful gift. If you want to read about the tensions caused by prophecy read Acts 21 a few times.

Want to know something really bizarre? Now I am a Pastor one of the first things I ask people coming to me with their problems is "What's your prayer life like? When did you last read your Bible?"

If you are ever in York as one of our city's 4.3 million visitors a year, why not get directions from our website and come and visit us? Then I can ask you about your prayer life too.

Maybe I will prophesy to you.

Most of all I pray that you might know the God that Rocky knows and that we know. He is a good God.

If you enjoyed this book or it helps you in any way, you can leave your comments at: www.notraining.eu